Ally to Adversary

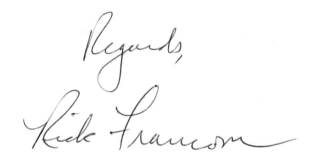

Larry,

Regards,
Rick Francona

ALLY TO ADVERSARY

An Eyewitness Account of Iraq's Fall from Grace

Rick Francona

NAVAL INSTITUTE PRESS
Annapolis, Maryland

Library of Congress Cataloging-in-Publication Data

Francona, Rick, 1951–

  Ally to adversary : an eyewitness account of Iraq's fall from grace / Rick Francona.

    p.   cm.

  Includes bibliographical references (p.) and index.

  ISBN 1-55750-281-1 (alk. paper)

  1. Persian Gulf War, 1991—Personal narratives, American. 2. United States—Military relations—Iraq. 3. Iraq—Military relations—United States.

4. Francona, Rick, 1951–   . I. Title.

DS79.74.F73   1999

956.7044'28—dc21   98-54464

Printed in the United States of America on acid-free paper ♾

06 05 04 03   9 8 7 6 5 4

For Emily,
who is everything I have tried to be

Contents

Maps

Foreword

Volumes have been written about Operation Desert Storm—accounts that analyze the events leading up to the war, the prosecution of the war itself, and postwar developments and consequences. These assessments range from military "lessons learned" reports to the Congress, including alleged U.S. intelligence failures, to geopolitical assessments attempting to gauge the impact of the war on regional relationships. However, it would be very difficult to find in any such source the same kind of interesting and insightful documentation of events that the reader will discover in *Ally to Adversary*.

In this very readable personal documentary, Lt. Col. Rick Francona chronicles critical events based on his unique personal experiences and unusual close-in vantage point. He makes no effort to analyze or take issue with critical military and political policy decisions, but rather he provides an extraordinary and personal description of events that allows the reader to draw his or her own conclusions.

The author's credentials are impressive indeed. He possesses a broad knowledge of the area based on his years of on-scene involvement. During the Iran-Iraq War, Lieutenant Colonel Francona walked the streets of Baghdad and toured battlefields while involved in a highly sensitive and successful effort to further American interests in the Gulf region. During that period, the author's unique expertise and access enabled him to provide U.S. officials with valuable insights into Iraqi military research and development efforts, efforts which were key to Baghdad's development and use of a variety of weapons systems, including ballistic missiles with the potential to carry chemical and biological warheads.

Also during this period, Lieutenant Colonel Francona developed personal relationships with Iraqi military officers in Baghdad and Washington. Described in this book is one such officer, Brig. Gen. Nabil Khalil

Sa'id—the Iraqi military attaché in Washington, who was later executed in Baghdad because of his close ties to the Americans. Another is Brig. Gen. Wafiq Al-Samarra'i, an intelligence officer who became the Iraqi director of military intelligence during Desert Storm and who later defected to the United States.

Prior to and during Desert Storm, the author was on the scene as personal interpreter for the commander in chief of the U.S. Central Command, Gen. Norman Schwarzkopf. In that capacity Lieutenant Colonel Francona observed the frustrations, failures, and successes experienced in both formulating and implementing policy and military planning decisions. This book provides interesting insights into the role of various agencies in Washington, including the Pentagon and the White House. The author includes his observations gained from active participation in a series of meetings in Washington as a member of the team dispatched by General Schwarzkopf to brief President George Bush, Secretary of Defense Dick Cheney, and the chairman of the Joint Chiefs of Staff, Gen. Colin Powell.

Ally to Adversary reveals special insight into the decision-making process relating to a range of key issues, including how to build an efficient coalition command and control structure, how to placate Saudi and Israeli sensitivities, when to launch an attack, and most importantly, when to terminate coalition military activity. Lieutenant Colonel Francona provides a comprehensive description of political and military effects of both the air campaign and the ground assault. He describes the difficulties in determining when, and indeed whether, to launch the ground offensive, including the need for accurate assessments of the damage inflicted by the air campaign. Once the tremendous success of the coalition air forces was apparent, the decision to launch the long-awaited ground campaign was "agonized over for days, even weeks." The factors influencing that decision are described hereby as partially military and partially parochial.

Lieutenant Colonel Francona was in Riyadh throughout the Iraqi missile attacks. In this book, he provides a vivid personal account of the impact of the attacks, the effect on the Saudis, the political crises resulting from the attacks on Israel, the defensive measures taken, and the role of intelligence in supporting the defensive effort. His description of the sequence of events regarding U.S. and Saudi cooperation—and at times the lack of cooperation—is both candid and illuminating.

The author's experience as a career air force intelligence officer coupled with his unique access to the Iraqis before, during, and even after Desert Storm allows him to shed considerable light on the strengths and weaknesses of the U.S. and coalition intelligence effort. It is an experience that basically counters the myth propagated by those who see a colossal intelligence failure in the provision of effective tactical support. Indeed, it confirms that for the most part, theater commanders in Desert Storm were provided with unprecedented and accurate details in the location of virtually every Iraqi division before and during the conflict. And yet Lieutenant Colonel Francona does expose the weaknesses of inadequate human intelligence assets to complement other intelligence systems. The book also describes incidents of parochial biases and traditional "rice bowl" concerns that continue to plague intelligence support to military operations.

It is obvious that the Middle East will continue to be an area of concern for America. Stability in the region is essential to U.S. national interests. But stability remains fragile indeed; the Middle East peace process continues to flounder. Saddam Husayn continues to lead a belligerent and defiant government in Iraq. Efforts to generate U.S.-Arab cooperation remains difficult as U.S. support for Israel remains a contentious issue. One thing is apparent—it is imperative that U.S. policy and military planners be as knowledgeable as possible of the past and current events and nuances that alter events in that area of the world. In that regard, *Ally to Adversary* is particularly informative and relevant reading.

LEONARD H. PERROOTS, Director,
Defense Intelligence Agency, 1987–89

Preface

From late 1987 until the end of the Iran-Iraq War in August 1988, the U.S. Department of Defense enjoyed a professional, cooperative relationship with the Iraqi Ministry of Defense. Yet by the end of 1988, that relationship had fallen apart, and we had started down a road that would end three years later in a tent on a desert battlefield in a place in southern Iraq called Safwan. I was a traveler on that road, both literally and figuratively, from Baghdad to Safwan. While there is not a great distance between these two locations—less than three hundred miles—it was one of the longest journeys of my life.

In Baghdad, I had sat with Iraqi military officers, worked with them during their war against the Iranians, enjoyed their Arab hospitality, visited their homes, and met their families. At Safwan in March 1991, not three years later, I sat with those same Iraqi officers, attempting to end another war—one that I had fought against them. How had it come to this?

The geopolitical situation in the Middle East was much different in 1988 than in 1991. In 1988, the specter of a militant Islamic government in Iran dominating the oil-rich Persian Gulf region was on the minds of senior U.S. officials. Iraq served as a convenient partner, if not ally. In the context of 1988, our cooperation with the Iraqi armed forces was the best option at the time. It was the right thing to do. Yet the deterioration of U.S.-Iraqi relations after the Iran-Iraq War was inevitable, given the nature of the Saddam Husayn regime and its use of chemical weapons on its Kurdish minority.

There are parallels to the situation in Afghanistan. Although the United States assisted the Islamist guerrillas, the Mujahidin, in their battle against Soviet occupation, the U.S. involvement was not about the Mujahidin; it was about the Soviets. Likewise, our cooperation with the Iraqis was not about the Iraqis but about the Iranians. Whereas the Mujahidin did not realize that fact, the Iraqis, a much more pragmatic people, understood completely.

Following the Iraqi invasion of Kuwait, and the commitment of U.S. forces to the defense of Saudi Arabia, it was natural for me to assume that I would be deployed to the Gulf. Arabic linguists were scarce, and Arabic linguists who had spent time in Iraq were even scarcer. On one hand, I felt honored to be selected to serve as General Schwarzkopf's interpreter, and I was anxious to deploy—after all, while no one wants to go to war, this is what I had been trained for, the reason I had spent years learning the difficult Arabic language. On the other hand, I knew I would be taking up arms against my former colleagues and friends. While the U.S. press was demonizing the Iraqis and the American military machine was gearing up for war, I felt a sense of loss and sadness. Iraqis whom I knew personally were going to die, and a city I had come to truly admire was going to become the target of American bombs and missiles—I had already been asked to provide targeting information on facilities in Baghdad. The coming war between Iraq and the United States was going to be personal for me.

I hope that I can offer some perspective on the events of the late 1980s and early 1990s and the changing relationship between Baghdad and Washington—an insight into how friend became foe. I have attempted to accurately portray events as I lived them, although I am sure many of the participants will have different recollections and perspectives, and undoubtedly many will have different opinions. On some occasions, I have omitted the names of persons involved for security or personal reasons. That fact certainly does not detract from these people's contributions. On other occasions, I may appear to be vague or not sufficiently descriptive. As a former intelligence officer, I am required to submit my writings to the Defense Department for a security review—some things must remain classified.

There was and is a Majid Al-Hilawi, although for his safety, I have chosen not to use his real name. He wears the uniform of the army of a country most Americans still consider to be the enemy. I was his colleague and friend; I ate at his table. I do not know where he is or how he has fared since that last day at Safwan, but I wish him well.

Acknowledgments

Many people have helped me turn a few anecdotes and "war stories" into a book. The initial encouragement to put down on paper the stories I had been telling since I returned from the war in 1991 came from my wife, to whom this book is dedicated. I was guided, cajoled, and encouraged by her and by many of our friends, who never seemed to tire of reading yet another draft.

I owe much in my career to Lt. Gen. Leonard Perroots, USAF (Ret.), who gave me a chance in 1987 to make a contribution to the conduct of U.S. policy in the Middle East. Maj. Gen. Jack Leide, USA (Ret.), arranged my assignment to Syria, the one job I had always wanted. I appreciate his faith in me during and after the war.

Col. Karl Polifka, USAF (Ret.), was responsible for my assignment as General Schwarzkopf's interpreter. When I started the book, Karl provided detailed accounts of events at the U.S. Central Command during the buildup to Desert Storm. Throughout the period of my working on the manuscript, he was a constant supporter, critic, editor, and sometimes taskmaster. Without his substantial input, this book would be incomplete at best—and, at worst, would probably never have been published at all. I have known Karl for fifteen years, and although we often have professional differences of opinion, he remains a mentor and close friend.

Lt. Col. Lloyd Tucker, USAF (Ret.), my first boss when I became a second lieutenant, taught me how to be an air force officer. The principles behind his often-exasperating correction of my writing seem to have finally sunk in. Col. Bernie Dunn, USA, provided frontline perspectives and details on coalition forces. He and his wife, Georgianne, were among the biggest cheerleaders for my writing the book. So were Col. Rick Pyatt, USAFR, and his wife, Maj. Zara Pyatt, USAFR, who never grew weary of hearing about my exploits. Maj. Ken Holtzman, USAF

(Ret.), added material and guidance based on his experiences as an interrogator of hundreds of Iraqi prisoners of war. Capt. Steve Long, USAF (Ret.), and his wife, Mary Jo, provided much-needed literary guidance and advice on how to say what I really meant, as opposed to what I had actually written, and how to structure the book. Col. Jim Ritchey, USA (Ret.)—the dean of military Arabists—taught me more about working with the Arabs than I ever learned from books.

Lt. Nick Eftimiades, USNR, insisted I keep writing when it would have been much easier for me to quit and not put up with endless revisions in my effort to get the manuscript to a publisher. Mark Gatlin, senior acquisitions editor at the Naval Institute Press, took a chance on an unpublished author. And many thanks to my editor, Dr. Gayle Swanson, for her dogged insistence that I do this right.

For their critical and objective reviews, I am indebted to Lt. Gen. Bernard Trainor, USMC (Ret.); Lt. Gen. Buster Glosson, USAF (Ret.); Brig. Gen. David Deptula, USAF; and Col. Tony Gain, USMC (Ret.). General Deptula's accounts and observations of the air campaign were especially useful.

And finally, I would be remiss if I did not acknowledge the efforts twenty-five years ago of the faculty of the Arabic Department at the Defense Language Institute, specifically Despina White, Rashad Wanis, Niniv Ibrahim, Alfi Yacoub, and Bahgat Malek. Without the language ability I gained through their hours and hours of instruction and individual attention, I would not have been able to take advantage of the unique opportunities that came my way. *Shukran jazilan.*

Acronyms

AFB	Air Force Base
AFRTS	Armed Forces Radio and Television Service
ATO	Air Tasking Order
AWACS	Airborne Warning and Control System
BDA	Bomb Damage Assessment
C3IC	Coalition Coordination, Communications, and Integration Center
CENTAF	Air Force, Central Command (USAF)
CENTCOM	Central Command
CIA	Central Intelligence Agency
CINC	Commander in Chief
CWO	Chief Warrant Officer
DCI	Director of Central Intelligence
DIA	Defense Intelligence Agency
DMI	Directorate of Military Intelligence
FROG	Free-Rocket-Over-Ground
FSTC	Foreign Science and Technology Center
GCC	Gulf Cooperation Council
GID	General Intelligence Directorate
GPS	Global Positioning System
HAS	Hardened Aircraft Shelter
HET	Heavy Equipment Transporter
HUMINT	Human Intelligence
IIS	Iraqi Intelligence Service
IMINT	Imagery Intelligence
IRGC	Islamic Revolutionary Guard Corps
JCS	Joint Chiefs of Staff
JFACC	Joint Forces Air Component Commander
JFC	Joint Forces Command

KKMC	King Khalid Military City
KTO	Kuwait Theater of Operations
MIMI	Ministry of Industry and Military Industrialization
MODA	Ministry of Defense and Aviation
NATO	North Atlantic Treaty Organization
NID	*National Intelligence Daily*
NORAD	North American Aerospace Defense Command
NSA	National Security Agency
OPEC	Organization of Petroleum Exporting Countries
OSD	Office of the Secretary of Defense
PGM	Precision Guided Munitions
RSAF	Royal Saudi Air Force
SANG	Saudi Arabian National Guard
SIGINT	Signals Intelligence
TEL	Transporter Erector Launcher
USAF	United States Air Force
USMC	United States Marine Corps
WATCHCON	Watch Condition

Ally to Adversary

The Arabian Peninsula and Persian Gulf region. *CIA*

Prologue

The real war will never get in the books.
Walt Whitman

SAFWAN, IRAQ—SUNDAY, 17 MARCH 1991
The three Iraqi officers were already seated when I escorted Maj. Gen. Robert Johnston, the U.S. Central Command chief of staff, into the negotiating tent at Safwan. The air in the tent was hot and oppressive, and it would get still hotter when tempers on both sides flared later during the meeting. The meeting had been requested by the Iraqis a few days earlier to discuss their declaration that they intended to move their fighter aircraft from dispersal and secondary fields back to their main bases. The aircraft were in essence trapped where they sat because of the coalition no-fly order imposed on Iraqi fixed-wing aircraft at the cessation of hostilities two weeks earlier. There would be little discussion—the answer was no. The marine two-star general attended the meeting to reinforce the seriousness of the no-fly order. If the Iraqis attempted to move their fighters, they would be shot down. Period.

The Iraqi delegation consisted of two general officers and their interpreter—a familiar face I had not seen for well over two years, Maj. Majid Al-Hilawi of the Iraqi armed forces Directorate of Military Intelligence (DMI). To say that I was stunned to see him would be an understatement; he seemed equally shocked. I was relieved to see that he had survived the war, since I knew that the Iraqi military intelligence headquarters compound had been bombed and severely damaged during the air war. In fact, I knew that the specific wing of the building that housed his office, where I had often sat with him, had been virtually destroyed.

3

Today we were sitting on opposite sides of the negotiating table, each armed and each wearing the uniform of our countries, now enemies. In an earlier chapter in Iraqi-U.S. relations, we had been colleagues. Actually, more than colleagues—we were friends.

"SHAKESPEARE WAS AN IRAQI"

The story of how Majid and I came to be friends and to face each other at Safwan that day began three years earlier, in 1988, and is closely tied to the history of the United States involvement with the Iraqi regime in the late 1980s.[1] Majid and I had first met in Baghdad during the Iran-Iraq War—or, as the Iraqis refer to it, the First Gulf War. We were both captains at the time, he in the Iraqi Army and I in the United States Air Force.

The geopolitical situation in the Middle East was quite different in late 1987 and early 1988 from what it was to be in 1991. By 1988, the Iraqis had been at war with the Iranians for almost eight years, with neither side able to end the carnage decisively. Two years earlier, in February 1986, in a series of bloody assaults, Iranian forces seized the Al-Faw Peninsula of Iraq, a desolate spit of salt marshes situated between Iran and Kuwait. Occupation of this piece of land allowed Iranian long-range artillery to shell Kuwait's northeastern oil fields in an attempt to intimidate the tiny sheikhdom.

Preparations were underway for the 1988 spring Iranian offensive, an annual operation timed to take advantage of the rainy weather and the muddy ground to offset Iraq's superiority in tanks and vehicles and to exploit the large numbers of Iranian volunteers willing to participate in massive human-wave infantry attacks. This year, however, the Iranians would start their offensive from the gates of Iraq's major southern city, the railhead and port of Al-Basrah. This was where the 1987 Iranian spring offensive was halted after a series of bloody assaults, often using thousands of fervent youths as human waves. As thousands of Iranians died in these offensives, so did thousands of Iraqi soldiers perish in the trench lines defending Al-Basrah. Loss of the strategic city could cause a general collapse of the Iraqi forces in the southern part of the country and possibly precipitate the loss of the war. The tenacity of the Iraqi soldiers in the defense of Al-Basrah—entire brigades were destroyed in the line—during the Iranian offensive of 1987 was to become a factor in U.S. military planning a few years later.[2]

A successful Iranian assault on Al-Basrah would likely lead to the one outcome deemed unacceptable by the United States: an Iranian victory. An Iranian success was very likely—Iraqi forces were faced with collapse in the Al-Basrah sector. Such an Iranian victory over Iraq would pose an immediate military threat to Kuwait, put incredible pressure on the other oil-rich Gulf Arab states to toe the Iranian line on oil production and prices, and limit the Gulf states' cooperation with the United States. Since the overthrow of Reza Shah Pahlavi and the coming to power of the Ayatollah Khomeini in 1979, a major Iranian policy goal had been the reduction of American influence in the Gulf region and the ability to raise crude oil prices. The Arab oil-producing states were the primary source of cheap oil for the United States and many of its allies. The United States considered the potential loss of access to Persian Gulf oil at reasonable prices a threat to its national security interests. Since the Carter administration in the late 1970s, successive American presidents made it clear that the United States would use military force to maintain access to Persian Gulf oil. A draw in the Iran-Iraq War was acceptable to the United States; an Iranian victory was not.

It was against this backdrop that I began my duties in Baghdad. The Defense Department developed a sensitive cooperative military-to-military relationship with the Iraqi armed forces in the aftermath of Iraq's mistaken missile attack on a U.S. Navy ship in 1987. On the morning of 17 May 1987, an Iraqi air force pilot fired two French-made AM-39 Exocet antishipping missiles against what he believed to be an Iranian tanker sailing in the Persian Gulf. The vessel was actually the U.S. Navy *Oliver Hazard Perry*–class guided missile frigate USS *Stark* (FFG-31). Thirty-seven American sailors died, and twenty-one others were wounded as a result of this missile strike. The Iraqi government made over twenty-seven million dollars in compensatory payments to the families of those killed in the attack.

To ensure that no other such error occurred on either side, members of the U.S. Defense Attaché Office of the U.S. embassy in Baghdad met regularly with Iraqi military officers to deconflict U.S. Navy and Iraqi Air Force operations, in essence assisting the Iraqis in their war against Iran.[3] The Iraqi military organization charged with conducting this effort with the United States was the Directorate of Military Intelligence.[4] The U.S. defense attaché and I met regularly with the Iraqi deputy director of military intelligence, Brig. Gen. Wafiq Al-Samarra'i.

Al-Samarra'i was in all respects a professional military intelligence officer; in fact, he went on to become the chief of the DMI during the Gulf War in 1991. In December 1994, he felt he could no longer serve under Saddam Husayn and defected to the Kurdish Democratic Party in northern Iraq.[5] Al-Samarra'i subsequently went to Turkey, to Syria, and finally to Jordan, where he became an outspoken member of an Iraqi opposition organization.

General Al-Samarra'i was assisted in this effort by a DMI interpreter, Capt. Majid Al-Hilawi. Majid had been selected to be our escort and interpreter because of his excellent command of the English language—he had obtained a degree in English literature from the University of Baghdad. He often tried to convince me that Shakespeare, his favorite author, was originally an Iraqi storyteller named Sheikh Zubayr (Az-Zubayr is the name of a city in southern Iraq) and that the writer's works were actually old Arab tales.

At a time when virtually all Iraqi males between eighteen and forty years of age were serving in the armed forces, Majid's position in the DMI was prestigious duty and was performed far from the front lines. Because of their involvement in the U.S.-Iraqi cooperative effort in 1988, Iraqi intelligence officers were exposed to American military doctrine and capabilities. Majid's familiarity with the American military and its capabilities, which he had gained during the period of U.S.-Iraqi military cooperation in 1987 and 1988, no doubt played a role in his assignment to the Kuwait Theater of Operations during operations Desert Shield and Desert Storm and in his presence at Safwan that day in March 1991.

My presence there the same day can also be directly attributed to that effort in 1988. Shortly after the United States deployed troops to Saudi Arabia in response to the Iraqi invasion of Kuwait in August 1990, the U.S. Central Command (CENTCOM) asked the Defense Intelligence Agency (DIA) to provide a military officer to serve as the personal interpreter for Gen. Norman Schwarzkopf, commander in chief (CINC) of CENTCOM. They asked for an officer with good Arabic language skills, preferably one with previous service in Iraq. Because of my participation in the military relationship between the Iraqi and American forces and the time I had spent in Iraq, I was considered the most qualified for the job. I was offered the opportunity, and I jumped at it.

Serving as the CINC's interpreter was to be the highlight of my career up to that point. At the end of the Vietnam War in 1973, I—along with hundreds of other Vietnamese-language interpreters—was offered a choice of other languages. At that time, the air force determined it had a need for linguists who could speak German, Hebrew, and Arabic. My choice of Arabic, which I made months before the oil embargo of late 1973, was to provide me years of interesting work that culminated in my involvement with the Iraqis from the efforts in 1988 through the end of Desert Storm in 1991.

As I sat on the plane bound for Riyadh and an uncertain future, I thought back to a more pleasant time in Baghdad in 1988 and to my colleague and friend Majid. Much had happened since then. The chasm between our countries had grown wider and deeper, and it appeared that war was on the horizon. At times it was difficult to believe that these two nations had once been able to cooperate as closely as they had. War had indeed made strange bedfellows. Now it appeared that we might take up arms against each other. I wondered when, rather than if, our paths might cross again.

1

Iraq 1988

THE ROAD TO BAGHDAD

Baghdad. The mere name conjures up thoughts of intrigue, mystery, danger, and evil. And rightly so. I was indeed to find all of these and more in the ancient capital on the banks of the Tigris River. The Arabic word from which the name Baghdad is derived means "to swagger, throw one's weight around, be fresh (properly, to behave like someone from Baghdad)."[1] Never was a city more aptly named.

By late 1987, Iraq had been at war with Iran for over seven years. After the fall of the shah in 1979, relations between Tehran and Baghdad deteriorated quickly. The new Iranian leader, Ayatollah Ruhollah Khomeini, called for the overthrow of Iraq's ruling Ba'ath Party and sanctioned several assassination attempts against senior Iraqi leaders. In 1979, Iran renewed its support to Kurdish and Shi'a separatist movements as well. The war, which began in 1980, drained both nations' economies and caused horrendous casualties.

Iraq, on the other hand, had sought to abrogate a four-year-old agreement that had established joint Iranian-Iraqi control over the Shatt Al-'Arab waterway, Iraq's only outlet to the Persian Gulf and the historical dividing line between two cultures, Arab and Persian. Sovereignty over the Shatt Al-'Arab had been a source of conflict between the two countries for years. In 1937, the international border had been set as the eastern bank except near the Iranian ports of Abadan and Khorramshahr, where Iranian port access was specifically guaranteed.

9

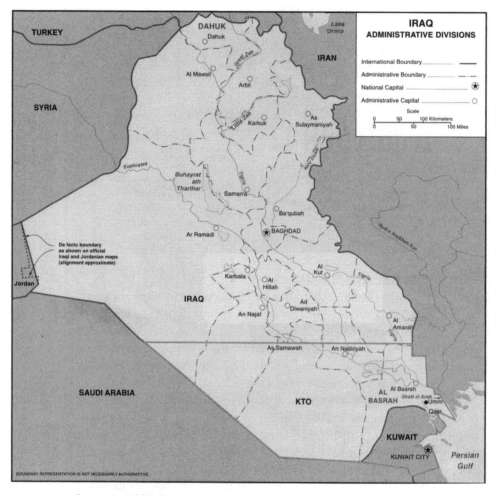

Iraq—in 1990–91 the outlined area in the bottom third of this map was designated the Kuwaiti Theater of Operations. *CIA*

Thus the agreement gave Iraq almost total control over the waterway and a lucrative source of income from tolls and fees. Iran unilaterally abrogated the agreement in April 1969 and challenged Iraqi authority. It also began support to the armed Kurdish separatist movements in northern Iraq.

On 6 March 1975, Iraq and Iran signed the Algiers Agreement (Iran-Iraq Treaty on International Borders and Good Neighborly Relations), brokered by Jordan's King Hussein. The agreement delineated the international border between the two countries as the thalweg, or the deepest point of the waterway, rather than on the eastern shore. Baghdad agreed to the treaty in return for Tehran's commitment to stop covert U.S. and Iranian support for the Kurds. The Kurdish uprising had exhausted the Iraqi army.

With Iran's military forces in disarray after the fall of the shah and purges of the Iranian officer corps, Saddam thought he had the military power to right the perceived wrong of his being forced to accept joint control of the Shatt in 1975. He also felt that his hand had been forced by Iran's recent covert actions. On 22 September 1980, Iraq launched a two-corps attack into Iran's Arabic-speaking Khuzistan province. After their initial foray into Iran stalled,[2] the Iraqis spent the next seven years on the defensive. By early 1988, it looked as though the Iranians might win the conflict.

Our participating in the cooperative effort between the U.S. Department of Defense and the Iraqi DMI meant our getting to Baghdad—not an easy feat in early 1988. Commercial air service into the capital had been virtually halted due to Iranian Scud missile attacks during the second round of the current "War of the Cities," the popular name applied to the exchange of Scud missile attacks on cities rather than military targets.[3] For reasons of secrecy and safety, use of U.S. military aircraft to travel to Baghdad was out of the question.

The preferred alternate route to Baghdad was a commercial airline flight to Kuwait, where we would meet the U.S. defense attaché, who drove an embassy vehicle down from Baghdad. In addition to allowing the attaché to observe Iraqi military operations in the roads between Baghdad and Kuwait, the trip also provided him an opportunity to stock up on supplies and food items difficult to get in war-weary Iraq. Early the next morning, we would begin the long drive north across the Kuwaiti desert, crossing the Iraqi border at Safwan, continuing north via Al-Basrah. From Al-Basrah, the route north took us through the area immediately behind the Iraqi front lines—from Al-Qurnah (where the Tigris and Euphrates meet to form the Shatt Al-'Arab) to the cities of Al-'Amarah and Al-Kut—and on into Baghdad. From Safwan to Baghdad, we were escorted by Iraqi DMI officers, who sped us through the dozens of military checkpoints on the way yet did not restrict where we went or what we saw. When we engaged in conversation with these officers, it became evident that they were proud of the performance of the Iraqi armed forces against the Iranians.

The drive from Kuwait to Baghdad required about ten hours and included many opportunities for close and sustained observation of the Iraqi army and its huge logistics machine at war. Although I did not realize it at the time, this intimate firsthand look at the Iraqi armed forces in a combat zone—a rare opportunity for an American military officer—provided me with an excellent foundation for understanding both the capabilities and limitations of an army that would some day face and engage American troops. I had studied the intelligence reports, read the books, and pored over the satellite photos, but it wasn't the same as being face-to-face with the reality. Reports and photos cannot impart the sounds, smells, heat, and grit, the sense of movement and the passage of time. As a wizened old master sergeant once told me, "There ain't nothing like being there."

The trip was a graduate course in Iraqi military capabilities. We had little information on how the Iraqis organized their logistics or how well they moved men and materiel from place to place. Compared to the transportation systems of other Arab countries I had visited, the infrastructure in Iraq was surprisingly well developed. Roads appeared to have been constructed to German autobahn standards; in fact, the signs were remarkably similar.[4] Rail terminals looked well maintained and efficient. Trucks and convoys appeared to be moving in an orderly fashion. Artillery batteries moved in columns with gun crews and gear in the cargo truck used to tow the weapons. All of the equipment looked as though it had seen plenty of use, yet everything appeared to be clean and serviceable.

All Iraqi military installations, from permanent facilities to temporary encampments, were marked with four- or five-digit cover numbers that were easily visible from the road. Unlike American military units, most Arab militaries do not mark the front entrance to their camps with their unit insignia and commander's name. Most have no identification at all. In order for the truck and the heavy equipment transporter (HET) drivers to reach the proper locations with a minimum of confusion, Iraqi military units were assigned a periodically changing unit designator, or cover number. The impression I formed was that of a well-oiled logistics machine, moving over a good road and rail system. Three years later, I would watch that system virtually collapse under the hammering of American air power.

While the southern front appeared to be all business, Baghdad in the spring of 1988 was a fascinating, vibrant, almost electric place that I grew to enjoy thoroughly. Admittedly, much of this impression stems from the fact that we were official guests of the Iraqi government. We were afforded preferential, often deferential, treatment. We were chauffeured everywhere in Mercedes sedans, traffic was halted by police officers to give us the right-of-way, and we dined at the best restaurants. Food appeared to be in good supply, although expensive for the average Iraqi, despite government subsidies financed by huge Iraqi loans from other Arab states and Western countries (including the United States).

It was a heady experience for a young air force captain. With the notable exception of the nightly Scud attacks and the occasional Iranian air raid, life was deceptively pleasant. The critical situation around Al-Basrah was two hundred fifty miles away, and the Iranians hadn't yet made their move. Although the second round of the War of the Cities was now in full swing, the situation was quite different from the first round: this time the Iraqis were winning, and they knew it.

Round one of the War of the Cities had taken place in the fall of 1987. Because of the range limitations of the Soviet-built Scud missiles used by both sides, Iranian Scuds were able to strike at Baghdad, but because Tehran was much further away from the border between the two countries, Iraqi Scud missiles launched from the border area could not reach as far as the Iranian capital. As a result, Iraqi missiles had to be launched against other cities closer to the border—not as effective as striking the capital itself. The situation was similar to that which the Iraqi Air Force had faced early in the war: Iraqi aircraft had to fly hundreds of miles into Iran to strike high-value targets, while most of Iraq's major targets were within a hundred miles of the border and vulnerable to Iranian air attacks. In the missile exchanges of 1987, the population of Baghdad felt defenseless and under siege.

The difference in the second round was the direct result of Iraqi engineering skill and a relentless quest for self-sufficiency. In 1988, Iraq's engineers proudly unveiled their first modified Scud missile. Iraq's project to modify the standard Soviet SS-1C Scud missile, known as Project 144, began in late 1986, with the first test launch taking place in the summer of 1987.[5] The new missile variant was called the "Al-Husayn," named for the Prophet Muhammad's son-in-law and a revered martyr of the Shi'a sect of Islam (and not for Saddam Husayn, as many have assumed). The Al-Husayn was a standard Soviet-produced Scud missile with a lighter warhead and increased fuel capacity. The warhead weight had been reduced from the original thousand kilograms to two hundred fifty kilograms. The lighter warhead and increased fuel allowed the Iraqis to double the range of the missile to over three hundred fifty miles and, for the first time in the war, to conduct direct missile strikes on Tehran. The tradeoff for the extended range was a less explosive charge and unstable aerodynamics, which resulted in less accuracy for an already inaccurate weapon system.

Iraqi print and broadcast media reported with great fanfare and relish the successes of the Al-Husayn missile. Each Iranian Scud impact in Baghdad was answered with four Al-Husayn launches. When round two of the War of the Cities ended in April 1988, Iraq had launched over two hundred Al-Husayn missiles; Iran had fired less than fifty Scuds. Unlike air strikes which the Iraqis had conducted against Tehran in the past, the missiles arrived with no warning. Because of the poor accuracy of the Al-Husayn as a result of the Iraqi modifications, they were fired at the city as a whole, not at specific military targets in the city. A hit anywhere in Tehran was considered a successful strike. It was a true weapon of terror. Despite relatively minimal damage caused by the small warheads, tens of thousands of Tehran's residents left the city for safer locations.[6] Three years later Israelis, Saudis, and American troops (me included) would come to know well the Al-Husayn and its successor, the Al-'Abbas.

As guests of the Iraqi military, our team was hosted at the best hotels in Baghdad. On the initial trip, we were put up at the now-famous Al-Rashid Hotel. Built to host the 1982 summit conference of the Non-Aligned Movement, it was both ostentatious and secure—and undoubtedly wired for audio and video surveillance of the guests.[7] The hotel had a fabulous pool and sports complex, its own helicopter pad, a bar that was frequented by Saddam's notorious sons, subways to other government buildings, and a large bunker/bomb shelter complex in the basement. A malfunctioning elevator once deposited us in the area of the bunker. Based on the numerous racks of sophisticated communications gear in that area, I suspect there was more under the Al-Rashid Hotel than we ever discovered. The Rashid was later hit by an American Tomahawk cruise missile that had been knocked off course by Iraqi antiaircraft fire. Today, the hotel is used to house United Nations inspection teams enforcing Security Council resolutions and journalists covering the crisis du jour.

That March, the nightclubs were packed as Iraqis celebrated their seeming victory in the War of the Cities. Favorite nightspots were the Nadi Yaqut (Sapphire Club) and the Khan Marjan, an ancient caravansary—a rest stop on the old caravan trade routes—converted into a restaurant and club. It was intriguing to watch the Iraqis, who after having endured over seven years of war were dancing and celebrating. Despite the brutality and repressive nature of the Saddam Husayn regime, I grew to like the Iraqis on a personal level and to respect their military capabilities on a professional level.

Although we were treated as special guests, the Iraqis took great pains to prevent us from roaming the streets alone. After all, we were declared American intelligence officers. We all knew that any cooperation between Baghdad and Washington was temporary and limited to a specific goal. The foundations and values of the two countries were far too different for a lasting relationship. We were not restricted in our movements but were escorted everywhere we went. On one visit during a free afternoon, I attempted to walk out of my hotel (the Palestine Meridien) and was immediately intercepted by a plain-clothes DMI warrant officer, who politely but firmly asked where I was going. I said I was going to the souk, an oriental bazaar, to buy a gift for my wife. He said he did not have a car that could take me there at that time but that maybe one could be arranged for later.

After thanking him for his "offer," I said that I knew where the souk was and would take a taxi. In a scene that reminded me of a Marx Brothers movie, he said, "Unfortunately, there are no taxis available now." Pointing to three cars—all painted in the distinctive orange and white pattern unique to Iraqi taxis—parked at a stand in front of the hotel, I remarked that any of these would do just fine. He walked outside and waved the drivers away. The drivers, conditioned not to ask too many questions of persons who appear to have authority, disappeared with their cabs. He turned and smiled, informing me that they must have been urgently needed elsewhere. Deciding not to give up, and feeling the need to respond to the challenge, I said that I needed to go to the embassy. He made a phone call, after which he told me he had arranged a car. A DMI car and driver took me to the embassy.

I walked into the embassy compound, out the back gate, and into the first cab I saw. I did not bother to determine if I was being followed; I just wanted to go to the souk and didn't care if the Iraqis knew that I was downtown shopping. I spent several hours wandering aimlessly through Baghdad's famous marketplace, talking to many shop owners and enjoying tea with others. Those who asked where I was from were thrilled to speak with an American, whose presence was an oddity at the time since there were no American tourists and very few U.S. officials in the country. Many were surprised that I could speak the language, and most assumed I was from one of the European countries that dealt with Iraq— the Soviet Union, Yugoslavia, France, Italy, Germany, to name a few.

When I returned to the hotel, the DMI warrant officer was standing on the steps. "You have been gone for over three hours," he said—by which he really meant, "You have been out of our control for over three hours." It became our secret; I knew he wouldn't tell if I didn't. As a CIA officer explained to me later, I fit the Iraqi counterintelligence and security services' profile of a case officer, an intelligence officer trained to spot and recruit foreign agents—in other words, a spy in Iraqi eyes. I was at that time thirty-six years old, a captain in the American intelligence service, and I could speak the local language—not someone the DMI wanted wandering the streets of Baghdad unescorted or unobserved.

For the most part, the Iraqi DMI officers were very gracious about making sure we saw the things we wanted to see in and around Baghdad, especially those things they wanted us to see. In 1988, despite over seven years of war—which included two rounds of the War of the Cities, Iranian air strikes, and a massive drain of resources—Baghdad remained a beautiful city. The Baghdadis were proud of their capital. Compared to the dusty capital cities of the Gulf countries, whose oil-wealth opulence appeared as just a facade, Baghdad had history, charm, and character. Unlike the situation in the Gulf cities where South Asians and Arabs from poorer countries performed most of the manual labor, in Baghdad most of the work was done by Iraqis. With the majority of the men serving in the armed forces, Iraq's women went to work in an effort reminiscent of that made by American women during World War II. Thus the character of the city remained Iraqi.

Visits to Iraqi war memorials were part of the excursions to cultural sites that our Iraqi hosts had arranged. For the most part, these monuments are tastefully done. The Tomb of the Unknown Soldier, with an eternal flame, is built in the shape of a large shield protecting a large Iraqi flag. Inside the memorial itself is a solemn war museum that portrays Iraq's battles with little of the expected anti-Israel (and often anti-U.S.) propaganda normally seen in Arab countries. On the other side of town is a beautiful monument to those who died in the Iran-Iraq War; it is called the Qadisiyah Martyr's Memorial. The name Qadisiyah was chosen for a reason: it refers to the battle in A.D. 635, in which an Arab army defeated an overwhelmingly superior Persian army, thus conquering the Persian Empire and introducing Islam to the area that is now Iran, Pakistan, and Afghanistan. The monument was built by the Japanese firm Mitsubishi and contains bronze tablets inscribed with the names of the dead. Here the propaganda machine is in high gear, detracting from the reverence that should be afforded the monument. Underneath the striking exterior of the memorial is a museum dedicated to the life of Saddam Husayn, including a family tree that purports him to be a direct descendant of the Prophet Muhammad. The story of Saddam's life as portrayed in the museum bears little resemblance to the actual truth.

I found the Iraqis an impressive people who had the appearance of being solid and tough. There were chinks in the armor of Iraqi stalwartness, however. Government control was evident everywhere. For example, while one could easily buy postcards at the Al-Rashid Hotel, one never saw any postage stamps there. I once asked the desk clerk for stamps, but she referred me to the post office. However, its location was unmarked on my tourist map because it was a government facility. After I found the post office, the clerk, seeing that I was obviously a foreigner, asked for my letter from the Ministry of Foreign Affairs authorizing the purchase of stamps for external mail.

The human impact of the restriction on mailing letters outside the country without special permission was driven home to me on a later trip when a young waitress at the hotel restaurant had trouble placing my Arabic accent (I am often told I speak Arabic with a Syrian-Lebanese accent). When I told her I was an American, she began to sob quietly and to tell me of her sister in Detroit, Michigan, with whom she could not correspond. She asked me if I could take a letter she had written to her sister and mail it once I had returned home. No one in her family was authorized to send overseas mail.

In a parallel situation, I tried to buy a new city map of Baghdad because one I had brought from Washington had taken a beating. At a local bookstore, I was told that maps were not authorized for sale because of the war, since they indicated the location of bridges and government buildings. The clerk said that even the maps that had been sold before the war contained intentional inaccuracies as a security measure.

For all of the bluster and party atmosphere in Baghdad, much of it based on the success of the Al-Husayn missile, the Iraqis were enjoying a false sense of security. The Iranians were massing at the gates of Al-Basrah and preparing for the attack. We could see it from our satellites. The Iraqis could not.

IRAQI DIRECTORATE OF MILITARY INTELLIGENCE

The principal organization in Iraq charged with monitoring the buildup of Iranian forces was the Directorate of Military Intelligence. The DMI was one of several intelligence organizations tasked with protecting the national security of the country. In the case of the government of Saddam Husayn, that meant collecting information that would eliminate any threat to the regime. The two major intelligence organizations were the Iraqi Intelligence Service (IIS), known commonly as the *Mukhabarat* (the Arabic word for "intelligence"), and the DMI. Other smaller organizations were the intelligence service of the Ba'ath Party and the independent intelligence organs of the two smaller military services, the Iraqi Air Force and Navy.

As in most countries, including the United States to some extent, the civilian intelligence service in Iraq focuses on major foreign policy and economic issues for the senior leadership. The military intelligence service collects information in response to the strategic, operational, and even tactical requirements of the Ministry of Defense and the armed forces. Again, as with most countries, intelligence collection outside Iraq is conducted using embassies as platforms for both IIS and DMI officers. IIS officers are usually assigned to the embassies, posing as Ministry of Foreign Affairs officers; DMI officers normally were assigned as military attachés.[8]

Unlike the intelligence services of the United States and most of its Western counterparts, the IIS and the DMI also have a domestic security mission. The primary mission of both the services is preservation of

the Saddam Husayn regime and the Ba'ath Party. To do this, both operate a wide range of informants inside and outside the country to collect information on Iraqis that may pose a threat to the regime. Both
have broad powers of arrest and employ coercive means to extract information and confessions from suspected dissidents. Assassination, torture, and terrorism are accepted tools of these agencies.

Following the initiation of hostilities with Iran in September 1980,
the DMI was forced to develop its skills to provide intelligence on Iranian
capabilities and intentions to the senior military leadership and field
commanders. It was a steep learning curve, but over the years the Iraqi
military intelligence officers developed a respectable capability against
the Iranians. Much of the information was gathered by human agents
(more commonly referred to as HUMINT, or human intelligence)
operating inside Iran. Southwestern Iran has a large Arabic-speaking
minority (the official language is Farsi), many with family, religious, or
other ties to Iraq. Some among this group of Iranians became active
intelligence agents for the Iraqis and provided a wealth of useful information. There were also those Iraqis and Iranians of the Shi'a sect of
Islam who had intermarried and, having moved between the two countries, were thus able to gather intelligence information through family
members still in Iran. Further, these Shi'a with ties in both countries
provided the DMI with a pool of potential operatives who could work
deep inside Iran to facilitate Iraqi attempts to overthrow first the shah
and later the Ayatollah Khomeini.

The DMI, over the years of the war with Iran, developed a good signals
intelligence (SIGINT) capability against Iranian tactical military communications. A series of Iraqi DMI communications-intercept sites monitored Iranian tactical communications and provided information
gleaned from them to field commanders. Although the Iraqi Air Force
had a fair photoreconnaissance capability, the Iraqis never developed
an appreciation for imagery intelligence.

The headquarters of the Iraqi DMI is located in the Kazimiyah section
of town, a Shi'a-dominated area in the northwest part of the city. The
area was named for the Kazimiyah mosque, a site holy to the Shi'a sect.
A modern walled compound had been built on the western bank of the
Tigris River to house the DMI offices. The offices of the director and
the deputy director, their staffs, and the communications center were
located in an administrative building. Across a courtyard was a multistory

analysis center. Other buildings included an officers club and a detention and interrogation facility.

The Iraqi director of Military Intelligence at the time was Maj. Gen. Sabr 'Abd Al-'Aziz Al-Duri. General Sabr had appointed his deputy, Brig. Gen. Wafiq Al-Samarra'i, to handle the contacts with the American defense attaché and me. Al-Samarra'i directed a dashing young captain to act as the officer in charge of making the day-to-day arrangements for the cooperative effort. That young captain, Majid Al-Hilawi, would be our primary contact in Baghdad. He soon became a personal friend. The Iraqi military attaché in Washington would be instructed to facilitate visas and travel arrangements to support the deconfliction arrangement with the Iraqi military.

The Iraqi military attaché in Washington at that time was Brig. Gen. Nabil Khalil Sa'id, the son of a well-known and respected Iraqi general as well as a war hero in his own right. Nabil enjoyed living in Washington and was an effective representative of his nation's military.

The differences in our two systems of government were illustrated by Nabil's amazement at the openness of American society. Nabil had acquired a pilot's license through the Iraqi Ministry of Defense, which owned all aircraft in Iraq. During one of our meetings, he asked me if it would be possible for him to fly while in the United States. I referred him to Jim Peak, the Defense Intelligence Officer for General Purpose Forces and an avid sports pilot. Jim discovered that Iraq had reciprocal aviation rights with the United States, so the holder of an Iraqi license could be issued a U.S. license by the Federal Aviation Administration. Jim arranged a license for Nabil and took him out to one of the many municipal airports in the Washington area. Nabil was amazed that the manager wanted to let him take an aircraft up immediately, without prior coordination from the local air force commander.

Nabil and Jim spread out a Washington-area flight map. Looking puzzled, Nabil asked, "Where are the restricted areas?" Jim began pointing out the rather small number of restricted areas—the White House, Camp David, and one or two others.

Nabil interrupted. "No, Jim," he said, "I mean the restricted areas where we can fly. In Iraq, there are small areas where you can fly, ten-kilometer [six-mile] circles."

"Nabil," Jim responded, "here you can fly anywhere you want." Nabil shook his head in disbelief.

While making arrangements to travel to Iraq, I became a regular visitor to Nabil's office in the Iraqi embassy near Dupont Circle. The chancery, despite its dignified red-brick federal style façade, was a fortress. To get to Nabil's office, I had to pass through four security posts. It appeared to me that everyone in the embassy was armed, including Nabil. After all, Iraq was a nation at war, and Washington has embassies or large populations of countries hostile to Iraq. Nabil was once detained at the main gate of a U.S. military base when a guard noticed a weapon in the car. Fortunately we were able to sort that one out easily. Since I was making regular visits to the embassy of a country on the State Department terrorism list, I was concerned that it might come to the attention of air force security or other counterintelligence agencies. Military officers cannot visit the embassies of such countries without authorization. Although I was conducting official business and was authorized to visit the embassy, I did not relish the thought of explaining what we were doing.

On the surface, cooperating with the Iraqis and coordinating American military operations with them sounds very straightforward; however, there were political realities involved. There were some senior officials in the U.S. government, especially in the Department of State, who were strongly opposed to our helping the Iraqis. Many State Department officials had served in Iran and had developed strong pro-Iranian and corresponding anti-Iraqi feelings.

The Defense Department effort would complement an ongoing intelligence relationship with Iraq. CIA officers had been dealing with the Mukhabarat for years, providing small amounts of low-level intelligence. That relationship expanded in 1986 and again in 1988.[9] The objective of the relationship was to prevent an Iranian victory—a victory that would allow the mullahs in Tehran to exert influence and control over the oil-rich Gulf Arabs. The term "oil-rich Gulf Arab states" usually includes Kuwait, Bahrain, Qatar, the United Arab Emirates, and Oman. However, the real meaning of the term in the context of U.S. national interests was then, is now, and likely will be for some time to come, the Kingdom of Saudi Arabia, with its over two hundred fifty billion barrels of proven oil reserves.

Given this unprecedented Iraqi access to U.S. intelligence capabilities, especially technical collection systems, we were not surprised three years later when we discovered that the Iraqis were purchasing commercially available satellite imagery from the French firm known as

SPOT (system pour l'observation de la terre) Image. The purchased imagery included shots of all the areas in Saudi Arabia that would be used by U.S. forces. That potential problem was resolved when the United States threatened to use a U.S. Army ground-based laser to blind the satellite if the French government did not limit the sales activity of the French company.[10]

In early April 1988, the Iraqis launched a coordinated two-corps (approximately seventy-five thousand troops) assault named Ramadan Mubarak (blessed Ramadan) that recaptured the Al-Faw Peninsula in thirty-six hours. During this operation, the Iraqis demonstrated what was to become a trademark tactic. The regular army forces in the area, in this case the VII Corps, were positioned on the front line to hold the enemy in place, while Republican Guard units, equipped with the best armor and artillery in the Iraqi armed forces, conducted the main assault. The regular army forces provided artillery fire and supporting attacks. After the Republican Guard had succeeded in breaching the enemy lines, the regular forces would move in to consolidate the gain. After the battle, the regular forces would assume occupation of the territory as the Republican Guard pulled back to move to the area of the next offensive.

The Iraqis conducted a focused air campaign that essentially broke the back of the Iranian military infrastructure in the southwestern part of Iran. This campaign paved the way for a series of Iraqi offensives in June and July (Shalamjah and the Majnun Islands) that brought the war to an end in August 1988. Interestingly, the Iraqi media began detailed coverage, to include gun camera footage, of Iraqi air strikes against Iranian facilities. I asked Majid why this activity was covered in such detail by state-owned media of a country that was obsessed with security and secrecy (I was careful not to phrase the question in exactly those words). He explained that the Iraqi pilots, both air force and army aviation (helicopters) pilots, had complained that the Al-Husayn missileers were getting too much credit for the Iraqi victories and they wanted their share of the glory.

During the war with Iran, Iraqi military planners realized that the Iranians had little to no aerial reconnaissance capability. As a result, the Iraqis inadvertently became complacent about camouflaging their military activities. This complacency, combined with the failure to understand American aerial and space-based reconnaissance capabilities, was to cause serious problems for them later. A case in point came in June

1988, when I was flying in an Iraqi army helicopter from Shu'aybah Air Base near Al-Basrah back to Baghdad. While flying over the confluence of the Tigris and the Euphrates Rivers at Al-Qurnah, I noticed hundreds of flat-bottomed military assault boats being stockpiled under and near the bridges over the Euphrates, easily visible from the air. Majid noted that I had seen what were obvious preparations for the upcoming assault on the Iranian-occupied Majnun Islands, and he asked the pilot to change course.

AL-FAW PENINSULA

It was during these offensive operations against the Iranians in the south and a counterinsurgency operation against the Kurdish minority in northern Iraq that a horrific Iraqi military capability was revealed—chemical warfare. Immediately after the recapture of the Al-Faw Peninsula, I was back in Baghdad to continue work on the cooperation effort, and I asked for a tour of the newly liberated peninsula area. The DMI arranged a flight on an armed Soviet-built Mi-17 "Hip" helicopter, a powerful workhorse used for air assault operations and general transport duties. This particular Hip had seen a lot of action, judging from the carbon deposits alongside its guns and rocket pods. The crew flew me (along with Majid) low and slowly from the DMI compound in Baghdad to VII Corps field headquarters just south of Al-Basrah.

Once we arrived, Majid introduced me to the corps intelligence officer as an American journalist. I was caught off guard by Majid's reference to me as a journalist, since U.S. intelligence community policy generally prohibits the use of journalism as a cover for operational activities.[11] The officer arranged a series of briefings by the VII Corps commanders who had fought the battle. One of the officers described Iranian tactics and, during an aside, talked about Iran's use of human wave attacks. The officer said that after watching hundreds, even thousands of Basij (Islamic Revolutionary Guard volunteers) being mowed down, Iraqi officers would climb onto tanks and use loudspeakers to implore the Iranians to stop having their own youths butchered. After the briefings and lunch, I was provided a four-wheel-drive vehicle and a driver and allowed free access to the battlefield, of course with Majid as my "guide."

Iraqi use of chemical warfare agents at Al-Faw was obvious. Strewn about the former Iranian positions and in the now-deserted command bunker and field hospital were used atropine injectors—some in standard NATO (North Atlantic Treaty Organization) green with U.S. military stock numbers and others, produced in Iran under license from a Dutch company, in a brown color. Atropine is used as the antidote for only one thing: nerve gas. Other observers who had toured the Al-Faw battlefields remarked that there were no birds in the areas and almost no insect life. As one would expect, the Iraqis officially denied any use of chemical weapons. While Iraqi and Iranian use of various forms of mustard (a blistering agent) had been known for some time, Iraqi use of extremely lethal nerve gas in combat was new and represented yet another success for the Iraqi military research and development establishment. We later learned that the Iraqis produced and used both Tabun (a nerve agent originally developed by the Germans during World War II) and Sarin nerve gases.

Iraq's much-publicized use of chemical warfare agents against the Kurdish village of Halabjah in March 1988 almost ended U.S. cooperation with Iraq and threatened the imposition of economic sanctions. Despite official Iraqi government denials that continue to this day, an Iraqi Air Force MiG-21 pilot defector admitted that he personally dropped two 250-kg bombs filled with nerve gas on the village, and other defectors have confirmed his story. Senior U.S. Defense Department officials became concerned that cooperation with a country that had used chemical weapons on its own citizens was politically indefensible in Congressional and public forums as well as morally reprehensible. However heinous the use of chemicals on the Kurds, the U.S. administration did not want an Iranian victory, so cooperation with Iraq—by both the CIA and the Defense Department—continued until the Iranians accepted a United Nations Security Council resolution to take effect in August, thus ending the war.

There were demands in Congress for sanctions on Iraq for its continued use of chemical warfare agents on its Kurdish minority. No serious demands for sanctions were made until the Iranians had indicated acceptance of a cease-fire with Iraq. The influential United States–Iraq Business Forum argued persuasively that sanctions imposed on Iraq would "reduce, rather than increase, our ability to influence Iraqi behavior."[12] Sanctions were not imposed, and over the ensuing year, U.S.-Iraqi trade reached almost four billion dollars. Aside from not wanting an Iranian victory, the administration was reluctant to deprive American companies of an important source of revenue.

While I was touring the battlefield at Al-Faw, one of my major objectives was to observe vacated Iranian positions. In moving from location to location, I was taken through numerous Iraqi fortifications and positions. Shots were exchanged with Iranian forces across the Shatt Al-'Arab, the waterway to the Persian Gulf separating the two countries. Iraqi artillery fired sporadically at the city of Abadan across the Shatt. As I traversed the Iraqi positions, I was able to observe from point-blank range Iraqi defensive doctrine: how they built their positions and laid out obstacles and minefields, what their artillery placement was, how many trench lines and fallback positions they had, what condition their weapons were in, what their morale was like, and so forth. I did not realize just how valuable a lesson I was learning. When the Iraqi invasion of Kuwait took place two years later, I was one of very few Americans who had been in Iraqi trenches during actual combat operations.

On the tour of the battle area, I was invited to visit a huge display of captured Iranian equipment. The Iranians had lost a cross section of their military inventory, and our examinations of the materiel contributed to our assessment of the Iranian forces. Simply examining maintenance records and inspecting the condition of the equipment yielded volumes of information about how the primarily American-trained Iranian armed forces were faring under the Khomeini regime. The Iraqis took great relish in pointing out huge piles of captured Iranian equipment that had been manufactured in Israel (Tadiran radios, Galil assault rifles, plus mortars and ammunition) and provided to the Iranians as part of the now-famous Reagan administration arms-for-hostages dealings with the Iranians. On more than one occasion, Majid and his fellow DMI officers asked if there was a Defense Department or CIA colleague of mine in Tehran working with the Iranians at the same time I was working with them in Baghdad. While the question was cloaked in humor, it was often delivered with some bitterness. They did not appreciate being treated as puppets on American strings.

Another thing struck me (although at the time it did not seem as important as it did in hindsight two years later) as I spoke to the Iraqi officers at VII Corps at Al-Faw that day: the disdain in which the Iraqis held the Kuwaitis. I noted that the Iraqi officers were watching Kuwaiti television. When I asked their opinion of the broadcasts as compared to those on Iraqi television, one of the Iraqi colonels pointed southwest toward Kuwait and said that someday they would teach a lesson to the "bearded women" who had watched Iraq bleed while defending the Arabs from the Iranians.

The human cost of the war, despite Iraqi actions to lessen the impact, was evident. Estimates of casualties on both sides exceeded a million dead and wounded. In proportion, Iraq's total number of almost four hundred thousand dead and wounded equates per capita to almost six million people for a population the size of the United States. In Baghdad, official notification of the death of a family member was not handled with the sensitivity attached to such a duty in the United States. It was not uncommon to see taxicabs, distinguished by their orange fenders, driving through the city with flag-draped coffins strapped to the roofs. The coffins were delivered to the families of the deceased soldiers with no prior notification. By 1988, the Iraqis were suspected of storing bodies from particularly bloody battles in a refrigerated morgue and releasing only a certain number each day in an effort to keep secret the number of casualties. It was the custom that a family who had lost a loved one place a black banner with the martyr's name and the date and place of death written on it at the corner of the main street nearest the residence. Reading the death banners allowed one to gauge the human cost of a particular battle. Families of soldiers killed in action received a car—usually it was a Brazilian-made Volkswagen Golf for the family of an enlisted martyr and an Oldsmobile Cutlass for that of an officer. (Usually the families sold these vehicles, thereby providing themselves with a kind of death benefit similar to U.S. "GI" insurance.) Amputees and those maimed in battle were normally assigned to military medical facilities far outside Baghdad.

PROJECT MORNING STAR

Our cooperative relationship with the Iraqis allowed us unprecedented access to the Iraqi military. For example, the Iraqis had captured a large artillery piece from the Iranians during the liberation of Al-Faw. They could not identify its origin and were perplexed by the unusual 170-mm bore. Artillery pieces worldwide are generally manufactured in standard bore sizes, normally 122-mm, 130-mm, 152-mm, 155-mm, 175-mm, and 203-mm. We knew they had captured this field gun: army colonel Gary Nelson—our newly assigned defense attaché in Baghdad and an artillery officer by training—had seen it while it was on display at a victory celebration in Baghdad. We knew what it was, and we wanted it.

The Iranians had acquired this self-propelled weapon in 1987. At that time, it was the longest-range field gun made anywhere in the world, capable of firing a rocket-assisted projectile to a range of almost sixty kilometers. It had been used by the Iranians to conduct harassment fire from the Al-Faw Peninsula into Kuwait's northeastern oil fields. The Iranians were applying military pressure on the Kuwaitis in a variety of ways, as punishment for supporting Iraq in the war and for alleged violations of oil export and pricing policies of OPEC (Organization of Petroleum Exporting Countries). This artillery fire was complemented by Chinese-made "Silkworm" cruise missile attacks on Kuwait's oil ports and by naval attacks on Kuwaiti shipping in the Gulf. The attacks were the catalyst for the March 1987 decision to register Kuwaiti oil tankers under the American flag (a procedure called "reflagging") to offer some protection for oil shipping in the region. The U.S. Navy could not legally protect foreign shipping, but a merchant ship flying the U.S. flag was entitled to armed navy escort through the Persian Gulf war zone.[13]

The high level of U.S. interest in the field gun had little to do with the situation in the Persian Gulf and rested instead on the fact that the gun had been designed half a world away to fire on the capital city of a close U.S. ally, South Korea. What the Iraqis had captured on the Al-Faw Peninsula, though they did not realize it, was a weapon designed and built by North Korea to fire on Seoul from the North Korean side of the Demilitarized Zone.

While inspecting the gun (the project was called Morning Star), we discovered more evidence of Iraq's use of nerve gas. As I rooted around the cramped driver's station of the gun system looking for anything of intelligence value—maps, notes, logs, manuals, firing tables, communications charts, and so forth—I found several used atropine injectors. These auto-injectors had been manufactured in Iran and were similar to those I had found earlier on a battlefield on Al-Faw. I showed one of the injectors (and pocketed another) to both Majid and the brigadier general commanding the artillery depot, explaining that these used injectors indicated to me that a nerve agent had been used at Al-Faw. I was careful not to accuse the Iraqis, but the implication was clear. The brigadier general replied that Iraqi artillery doctrine calls for use of obscurant smoke in the preparatory artillery barrages. His "analysis" was that the Iranians mistook the smoke rounds for nerve gas and, therefore, self-administered atropine. Not wanting a confrontation while standing in the middle of an Iraqi military installation, I did not mention to the Iraqi officers that we had also discovered decontamination fluid in many places on the weapon, most noticeably trapped in the headlights. It would make no sense for the Iraqis to decontaminate the vehicle if they had only fired smoke rounds at the Iranians.

"IN GOD WE TRUST"

On 25 May, during that same trip, the Iraqis launched an offensive named Tawakalna 'Ala Allah (in God we trust) against Shalamjah, an area just north of Al-Basrah and east of the Shatt Al-'Arab, then occupied by the Iranians. As in the Al-Faw offensive, the Iraqis pushed the Iranians out of Iraqi territory back across the international border, but unlike Al-Faw, they met stiff resistance from the Iranians and paid a high human price for the land. The successful recapture of this area secured the still-vulnerable eastern approaches to Al-Basrah. We noted that there were an unusually high number of black banners in the poorer Shi'a sections of Baghdad bearing the words "Martyred at Shalamjah."[14]

During the cleanup of the battlefield, I flew with the Iraqi Air Force to their air base at Shu'aybah just west of the area of the battle. While a group of Iraqi officers (including Majid) and I were driving north of Al-Basrah near Shalamjah to survey captured Iranian equipment, the Iraqis removed scores of their damaged tanks and armored personnel carriers from the battlefield. There was a steady stream of ambulances and dozens of coffin-laden trucks as well. The Iraqi officers with me appeared uncomfortable that I had witnessed evidence of heavy Iraqi casualties, understanding that I was reporting my observations back to Washington.

Between March and July 1988, I made a total of six trips to Baghdad. Four of these trips roughly coincided with major Iraqi offensives against the Iranians along the southern border between the two countries, each new offensive further north than the previous one. On 18 July 1988, the Ayotollah Khomeini announced that Iran would accept the terms of a United Nations Security Council resolution ending the war.

In addition to the crushing defeats they suffered in battles against the Iraqis, another factor may have influenced the Iranians to accept the cease-fire. Two unrelated incidents earlier in 1988 involving the U.S. Navy may have caused the mullahs in Tehran to think they were fighting more than just the Iraqis. On 14 April the guided missile frigate

USS *Samuel B. Roberts* (FFG 58) struck an Iranian mine in the Gulf while escorting reflagged Kuwaiti tankers. In response the U.S. Navy conducted Operation Praying Mantis, in which two Iranian oil platforms in the Gulf used as observation posts to coordinate attacks on merchant shipping were destroyed by naval gunfire. During the execution of the operation, the Iranian navy attempted to challenge the American task force. When the conflict was over, three Iranian warships had been sunk or destroyed, and six more Iranian armed speedboats had been put out of action.

On 3 July 1988, the guided missile cruiser USS *Vincennes* (CG 49) mistakenly shot down an Iran Air commercial airliner, killing two hundred ninety passengers. Despite official claims to the contrary and a generally good understanding of American ideals, Iranian military officers with whom I have spoken believe that the United States deliberately downed the plane to send Tehran a message that the United States would intervene in the war to ensure that Iran would not win. Three weeks after the incident, Tehran accepted the cease-fire. The United Nations resolution went into effect on 20 August 1988. The battle lines were about where they were in September 1980 when the war started. Iranian and Iraqi national treasures totaling over a trillion dollars had been squandered, and a human toll of over one million dead or wounded had been suffered in vain.

When the war was over, the Iraqis put on a massive display of captured Iranian weapons in Baghdad. The numbers were astounding—the Iraqis had captured almost 75 percent of Iran's armor and artillery. Although territorially the eight-year war can be considered a draw, on the field of battle in 1988 the Iraqis had prevailed. A military analyst would draw the conclusion that the major cause of the Iranian defeat was the systematic destruction of Iran's logistics infrastructure and command and control system and, conversely, Iraq's preservation of its robust logistics infrastructure and command and control.

The Iraqi success was directly attributable to the decision made in Washington to provide U.S. intelligence information to Baghdad and to cooperate with the Iraqi military. However, senior Iraqi officers failed to appreciate their unique insights into American intelligence capabilities and American military operational capabilities. This failure was to be a contributing factor in the Iraqi defeat at the hands of an American-led coalition not three years later.

My last trip to Iraq as part of the deconfliction effort was in September 1988. This time the atmosphere was dramatically different. No nights out on the town, merely a quiet dinner in the DMI compound. Conversations were very subdued, and even Majid was never alone with me. Another DMI captain was assigned to escort me, even when I was with Majid. I wondered whom he was watching—Majid or me. Now that the mission had been accomplished, any further or unnecessary association with me was suspect, and in Iraq, suspicion was the same as guilt. As we concluded the final office call, the Iraqis assumed their normally stoic posture and said a formal—and what we all knew was a final—good-bye.

Majid was able to arrange a private dinner, probably at some risk to himself, at his apartment in Baghdad. He told me that he had been ordered not to escort us to the airport the next day, that the other captain would be there instead. We assumed that with the end of the war and threat of an Iranian victory eliminated, Washington and Baghdad would resume the strained relationship based on Iraq's beliefs that American Middle East policy was unbalanced in favor of Israel. I thanked Majid for all the personal things he had done for me during the past six months, especially the trip to his native Babylon, of which he was justifiably proud. We couldn't have been more different—he from the desert between the Tigris and the Euphrates Rivers and I from the steel country of western Pennsylvania—but we had done something momentous together. After a final Arab embrace, I departed, fully expecting never to see him, or Iraq, again.

As the Iraqi Airways jet lifted off from Baghdad's Saddam International Airport the next morning, the Defense Department's relationship with the Iraqi armed forces ended. Now, years later, it remains controversial.

2

Interregnum

Soon after Iran accepted the United Nations resolution ending the fighting with Iraq in August 1988, Iraq was faced with a series of challenges. With the end of combat operations came pressure to release thousands of Iraqi men from military service, men who wanted jobs and a return to their place in society. However, eight years total dedication to the war effort had caused fundamental changes in Iraqi society as well as in Saddam Husayn's views of Iraq's destiny. These two forces would eventually clash and, to a great extent, shape the future of the region.

As the days of celebrations came to an end in Baghdad, signs of change were beginning to be visible. Small numbers of soldiers were released from military service. The regime chose a slow rate of demobilization to prevent a sudden influx of young men into an economy that did not have the capacity to absorb them. The situation was exacerbated by conditions unlike those in most of the Arab world. During the eight years of war against Iran—a country with three times Iraq's population base—virtually all able-bodied Iraqi men served either in the armed forces or with other government organizations. This led to the widespread employment of women in both the private and the public sectors. Unlike their Arab sisters in the Gulf, Iraqi women took a variety of jobs and found that they enjoyed the new way of life.[1] Many of these women were reluctant to give up their newfound careers to make way for the returning soldiers. Faced with the prospect of having thousands of unemployed men with years of combat experience growing disenchanted in the streets, Saddam chose to limit the number of soldiers being demobilized.

Despite the slow rate of demobilization, the signs of war's end were evident. Antiaircraft guns were removed from the roofs of public buildings, and hundreds (but not all) of police and security service checkpoints were dismantled. Travel became easier, and food prices decreased. More to the point, however, cooperation with the United States ceased virtually overnight. The short-term national security interests of both countries had been met. Iraq, with some help, had forced the Iranians to accept a cease-fire, and the United States had achieved its goal of preventing Iranian hegemony in the Gulf.

The newly arrived U.S. ambassador, April Glaspie—an Arabic-speaking career foreign service officer with extensive experience in the Middle East—was held at arm's length by the Iraqi government. She was prohibited from moving around freely and was unable to develop meaningful contacts in the Iraqi government. As far as the Iraqis were concerned, the United States was once again the primary sponsor of Israel, and its assistance was no longer needed or wanted. On the American side, reports of Iraq's use of chemical weapons against Iranian troops and its own Kurdish minority had soured many U.S. officials, particularly in the State Department, concerning any relationship whatsoever with the Iraqis.

The tactical alliance was over. That fact was signaled to Baghdad clearly by the U.S. State Department. On 8 September 1988, Iraqi Foreign Minister Sa'dun Hammadi was scheduled to meet with Secretary of State George Schultz. The Iraqis, who had been careful to make all their payments of U.S. agricultural loans, hoped to maintain good relations on the trade and industrial level. However, their hopes were dashed when the State Department spokesman called a press conference two hours before the Schultz-Hammadi meeting and stated, "The U.S. Government is convinced that Iraq has used chemical weapons in its military campaign against Kurdish guerrillas. We don't know the extent to which chemical weapons have been used but any use in this context is abhorrent and unjustifiable. . . . We expressed our strong concern to the Iraqi Government which is well aware of our position that the use of chemical weapons is totally unjustifiable and unacceptable."[2]

For years, various Arab leaders have espoused the tenet that the individual Arab states make up one "Arab nation." In Baghdad, Saddam now viewed Iraq—and thus himself—as the leader of this Arab nation. Certainly he possessed the dominant military force in the area, second only to Israel. Having been humiliated by the 1981 Israeli air strike on his nuclear research facility at Osirak, Saddam was well aware of Israel's military power and its ability to project that power. He also was aware of Israel's nuclear capability. At the end of the Iran-Iraq War, Israeli military planners considered Iraq the number one threat to its security. Given the competence with which the Iraqi armed forces had planned and executed a series of complex military operations against the Iranians in 1988, many analysts believed the Israelis were correct in their assessment.

When the war ended, Iraq had over one million men under arms—most with some combat experience, and many with years of it. The Iraqis were now the world's premier nation in the employment of chemical munitions as an integral part of a battle plan. Iraqi pilots flying French- and Soviet-built advanced fighters were skilled in the delivery of precision-guided munitions, albeit against relatively weak Iranian air defense capabilities. Iraq had not only purchased state-of-the-art self-propelled and towed field artillery guns from France, Austria, and South Africa but had also modified Scud short-range ballistic missiles that gave it the ability to strike far from its borders. Additionally, Iraq possessed enough HETs to move the tanks and armored personnel carriers of an entire armored corps (three heavy divisions, or over fifteen hundred tanks and combat vehicles) in one operation, a capability not lost on U.S. military analysts. During the latter stages of the war with Iran, Iraqi logistics officers moved entire divisions from one end of Iraq to another in twenty-four hours, distances of four hundred miles or more. These are standards worthy of any modern army.

Rather than large-scale demilitarization, Saddam embarked on a costly program of increasing his already sizable weapons research and development programs and military industrialization efforts. This was coupled with attempts to portray Iraq in a favorable light around the world through cultural projects, such as the restoration of the ancient city of Babylon. The magnificent blue Temple of Bel, more commonly known as the Gate of Ishtar, built during the reign of Nebuchadnezzar II in the sixth century B.C., still stands. Nebuchadnezzar was one of Saddam's heroes, having destroyed the city of Jerusalem and the Jewish Temple in 587 B.C. With United Nations and international funding, Iraqi archaeologists completed major excavation of the ruins of Babylon, unearthing many of the original foundations and city walls. Made of mud bricks, a great number of these structures bore the still-legible seal of Nebuchadnezzar. To the dismay of the world's archaeologists, Iraqi workmen began reconstruction of the city directly on these original foundations, this time with mud bricks bearing the seal "in the era of Saddam Husayn."

Iraqi weapons research projects were under the control of a rising star, Lt. Gen. Husayn Kamil Hasan Al-Majid, head of the Ministry of Industry and Military Industrialization (MIMI). Husayn Kamil was a son-in-law and distant cousin of Saddam Husayn. The story of Husayn Kamil is well known. He rose further in the Iraqi hierarchy to become minister of defense and later the director of the Organization of Military Industries, the element responsible for all of Iraq's advanced weapons efforts.

On 8 August 1995, Husayn Kamil defected to Jordan with his brother and their wives—both Saddam Husayn's daughters. Both men were killed in Baghdad after they returned to Iraq and attempted reconciliation with Saddam Husayn less than a year later. Husayn Kamil's return to Iraq on 20 February 1996 ended a strange chapter in Iraqi internal politics. Both men had done well in the Iraqi regime and owed their success to Saddam. Why they returned to Iraq remains the subject of speculation, but persistent reports indicate that Saddam Husayn offered to spare the lives of their relatives and extended families in exchange for their return (and the return of his two daughters) and certain execution. Press reports claimed that the Al-Majid family killed the two brothers to restore their honor, and Saddam's eldest son 'Uday claimed that Husayn Kamil committed suicide.[3] In truth, however, they were killed in a pitched gun battle with officers of the Iraqi Special Security Organization (SSO). After the Sunday morning firefight, the bodies of the two brothers were dragged through the streets. One of several children killed in the shooting was Saddam Husayn's grandson.

Husayn Kamil was responsible for Iraqi successes in the modification of the Soviet Scud missile to the Al-Husayn missile, and the capability to produce the nonpersistent nerve agents Tabun (known by its chemical warfare designator, GA), Sarin (GB), and Soman (GF). These agents were gaseous and evaporated or dissipated quickly in the atmosphere. Iraqi scientists, under Husayn Kamil's leadership, developed ever more lethal forms of nerve agents, including VX—a liquefied and persistent agent, the most potent in the U.S. and Soviet arsenals.[4] Iraqi chemical engineers, trained in the best universities of Europe and the United States, had also developed a dusty form of mustard, which is usually employed as a gas or a liquid. This dusty mustard is said to be able to penetrate the charcoal-lined U.S. chemical protective suit.[5]

Among MIMI's other successes was the modification of transport aircraft to carry air surveillance radar, giving Iraq a rudimentary AWACS (airborne warning and control system) capability. The engineers also added aerial refueling capability to many of its Soviet-built jet fighters (the French-built fighters were delivered from the factory with aerial refueling capability). Iraqi capability to modify aircraft was well-respected. Iraqi engineers had installed a fighter aircraft radar system and AM-39 Exocet missile launchers on a French-built Falcon 50—far beyond the capabilities afforded them in assessments prepared by many Western intelligence services.

The innovative weapons designs and methods employed by Iraqi engineers stunned Western observers at an arms exposition in Baghdad in early 1989. Many of the modifications were crude but effective. Iraq displayed its full range of missiles, modified aircraft, and indigenously produced armor, artillery, and rocket launchers. The question asked by many Western political-military analysts was whether Iraq was producing military hardware in hopes of selling it to its Arab brethren and other third world countries, or was Iraq embarking on a program of self-sufficiency and sustainment in case it faced the type of embargoes applied to other pariah states (such as the former Rhodesia and South Africa).

In 1989, Saddam Husayn not only sought to develop an indigenous weapons production capability but also began to involve Iraq more in regional affairs. He sought to establish ties with Christian groups in Lebanon, to the point of providing weapons to the groups, including an attempt to ship Scud missiles. In February of that year, Iraq joined Egypt, Jordan, and the Yemen Arab Republic in forming the Arab Cooperation Council, a grouping of otherwise pro-West Arab states. This group consisted of countries not rich in oil, possibly as a counter to the economic power of the oil-rich states of the Gulf Cooperation Council (GCC). Formed in 1981 to foster Gulf Arab political, economic, and military cooperation, the GCC includes Bahrain, Kuwait, Oman, Qatar, Saudi Arabia, and the United Arab Emirates.

Against this backdrop, Ambassador Glaspie remained of the same mind as many of us at the Pentagon, particularly in the DIA. We believed that Iraq was too important a player in the region to ignore. Saddam Husayn possessed the world's fourth largest (and possibly most experienced) armed forces as well as chemical weapons and the means to deliver them to any of his neighbors. The Iraqis were clearly the dominant military power in the region, second only to Israel. Glaspie remarked to U.S. Central Command (CENTCOM) commander in chief, Gen. H. Norman Schwarzkopf, that ignoring Iraq "would be like denying cancer."[6] She proposed that CENTCOM—the command responsible for U.S. military operations in southwest Asia (including most of the Middle East) and part of east Africa—try to reestablish military-to-military contacts with the Iraqi armed forces. Since Iraq was a military state, she saw this as a possible means of gaining access to Iraqi inner circles or a method to exert influence on Iraq. The idea was firmly quashed at the State Department in Washington, and we at the Pentagon were told not to discuss it further.

Iraqi engineers surprised the world in December 1989 with the launch of the Al-'Abid (Servant of God) space-launch vehicle test bed. A year after Israel had placed its first Ofeq research satellite in orbit, Iraqi engineers demonstrated the capability to simultaneously ignite five liquid-fuel Scud-type rocket engines. The launch was a test of the first stage of a three-stage system; the second and third stages were inert. This test explained Iraq's earlier detected attempts to acquire American-made precision switches needed for missile stage separation (as well as precise detonation of high explosives in a nuclear implosion device). All of Iraq's missiles up to this point were single-stage designs. Although billed as a space-launch test bed, the vehicle generated sufficient thrust to power a twelve-hundred-mile-range missile, as claimed by Saddam Husayn during press coverage of the event. The link between the so-called space-launch vehicle project and a medium-range missile was unmistakable. Video footage of the launch console clearly identified the effort as Project 144/5, an obvious outgrowth of Project 144, the conversion of Soviet Scud missiles to longer-range Al-Husayn missiles two years earlier. The publicity afforded the launch was meant to send a message to Iraq's primary foe, Israel.

That message was reinforced not three months later in February 1990 when U.S. intelligence detected the construction of twenty-eight

Scud-type missile launchers in five complexes in western Iraq. The fixed launchers were positioned in an unusual northeast to southwest pattern, with the launcher arms positioned to fire in a west-southwesterly direction. Assuming that these fixed launchers were for Al-Husayn or similar class missiles, arrangement and location of the launchers suggested that the targets were the Israeli cities of Tel Aviv and Haifa and the nuclear research facility at Dimona. The assessment of targets was fairly straightforward—one of the limitations of the Al-Husayn modified Scud was its fixed range of about three hundred fifty miles. Firing at a target required that the launcher be positioned at the appropriate distance; no change in the range of the missile was possible. Drawing an arc on a map indicating the range of the missile revealed the target options. Missiles launched from these complexes could also strike Syria and Turkey.

This raises the question—why place fixed launchers so obviously targeted at Israeli cities and facilities in easily visible and detectable locations? No one but Saddam Husayn knows for sure, but many observers who have studied the enigmatic Iraqi leader believe he was trying to create a strategic deterrent to Israel's perceived nuclear arsenal. It appeared that Saddam was trying to replicate, albeit on a much smaller scale, the U.S.-Soviet paradigm of mutually assured destruction. It was widely speculated that Iraq had developed a nerve-agent warhead for the Al-Husayn family of missiles. That speculation was confirmed during a vitriolic anti-Israel speech on 2 April 1990 when Saddam claimed that Iraq did in fact possess binary chemical warheads for the missiles and that he would use them to "burn" Israel. Computer models of the detonation of just one Al-Husayn chemical warhead over Tel Aviv postulated as many as eight thousand deaths. Use of biological agent warheads would be even more lethal. Israeli planners now had to face the reality that attacks on Iraq could result in a chemical or perhaps a biological warfare response. CENTCOM declared Watch Condition (WATCHCON) IV, signifying a potential threat to U.S. citizens, interests, or operating forces.

Following Husayn Kamil's defection in 1995, Iraq released tens of thousands of pages of data to the United Nations Special Commission containing more details of its advanced weapons programs of the late 1980s and early 1990s. The Iraqis assumed that the former chief of MIMI would reveal it to Western intelligence agencies anyway. As such, the details of Project 144/2, the development of chemical and biological missile warheads, were revealed. In addition to fifty chemical agent Scud warheads (some filled with VX, others with Sarin), the Iraqis admitted the existence of 157 aerial bombs and twenty-five Scud/Al-Husayn missile warheads filled with the biological warfare agents anthrax, botulinum toxin, and aflatoxin. Stockpiles were declared to include eighty-five hundred liters of anthrax, nineteen thousand liters of botulinum toxin, and twenty-two hundred liters of aflatoxin. To put eighty-five hundred liters of anthrax into perspective, a fatal dose is one-millionth of a gram, and it kills in five to seven days, nearly 100 percent of the time. Botulinum toxin can kill in as little as twenty-four to thirty-six hours by paralyzing the respiratory system. Aflatoxin is a liver carcinogen that can kill years after ingestion.[7] Iraq's stockpiles at the outset of Desert Storm were more than sufficient to wipe out the human race several times over.

Additional Iraqi weapons engineering expertise was revealed when British and U.S. customs uncovered a sophisticated Iraqi clandestine purchasing network operating in Europe and the United States. This network had acquired metallurgical furnaces and components for centrifuges made of maraging steel (a high-technology alloy needed to build centrifuges capable of handling the dense metals used in the development of weapons grade fissile material). The attempt to acquire maraging steel—coupled with the attempt to buy switches needed for precision detonation of high explosives in a nuclear implosion device—pointed to a nuclear weapons program more advanced than the U.S. intelligence community had estimated. The intelligence community's conclusion that Iraq would need ten years to develop a nuclear device was too conservative. Information gained from United Nations inspections following operation Desert Storm prompted a revision of that estimate: Iraq could have developed a nuclear weapon in two to five years, had the program not been interrupted by the war.

In February 1990, the Iraqi regime did itself no favors when it executed an Iranian-born British journalist, Farzad Bazoft, on charges of espionage. After the execution, the body was unceremoniously dumped at the British embassy. Such actions only strengthened many American officials' opinion of Saddam Husayn's Iraq as a regime of thugs.

On 10 April 1990, British customs agents seized giant artillery components (labeled as oil pipes) for a 1,000-mm bore "super gun" designed to fire chemical or high-explosive warheads hundreds of miles—far enough to strike Israel. Using concepts abandoned by U.S. engineers in the 1960s in favor of missile technology, Iraqi super-gun developers undertook what was known as Project Babylon. Canadian engineer Gerald Bull served as the project's director until his murder in Belgium on 22 March 1990, less than three weeks prior to the British customs seizure. Although the perpetrators were never apprehended, many people believe that the Israeli intelligence service, the Mossad, was responsible.

After the war, United Nations inspectors discovered a completely assembled 350-mm gun with a barrel 172 feet long at Jabal Hamrayn, in the remote mountains of northern Iraq some one hundred miles north of Baghdad. The barrel of the weapon was aimed to the west— at Israel. Analysts speculated that the large gun had been built in the remote mountainous area to prevent detection by U.S. reconnaissance satellites. Components for the 1,000-mm gun that had earlier escaped British customs detection were found at a location about thirty miles south of Baghdad. The Iraqis admitted to the United Nations inspectors that these guns were designed to deliver nuclear, chemical, and biological warheads.[8] Husayn Kamil said in an interview with CNN that the gun was also designed to blind reconnaissance satellites.

The war with Iran was over, yet Iraq continued its attempts to build a vast arsenal of advanced weapons, including chemical and nuclear weapons. These weapons could be carried far beyond Iraq's borders by either long-range ballistic missiles or aircraft capable of aerial refueling. Neither the Iraqi economy nor its infrastructure could support the level of spending in weapons research and development or procurement, but Saddam stayed the course. Eventually, military spending would need to be reconciled with the economy. Israel and the United States grew more and more concerned as to how that might take place. So too did Iraq's Arab neighbors.

3

Prelude to Conflict

By 1990, relations between Iraq and virtually all of its neighbors had reached an all-time low. Saddam Husayn had unsuccessfully attempted to extort new loans from the oil-rich Gulf Arabs, who he felt were indebted to him for Iraq's defense of the "Arab nation" against the Iranians during the Iran-Iraq War. To make matters worse, he refused to repay existing loans from these countries. He had borrowed heavily from these Arab states during the war and was now faced with a total of over eighty billion dollars in debts. This figure included thirty-seven billion to Arab countries, primarily the members of the GCC, and another ten billion to Kuwait alone. These states were reluctant to write off or reschedule the existing loans, let alone make new ones. Iraq's annual debt service on the twenty-three billion owed to just the Eastern European and Far East states—Baghdad's primary weapons suppliers—would consume over one half of its annual oil revenues. This debt did not address the money owed to the West, including the United States. While Iraq defaulted on many of its loans from the Arab states, Baghdad made all of its payments to American banks to ensure that U.S. Department of Agriculture Commodity Credit Corporation purchases were not endangered.[1]

Increasing spending on its military research and development efforts exacerbated Iraq's already dire financial situation. When asked for a financial grant by Saddam, the emir of Kuwait responded with an offer of a small long-term loan. Relations immediately took a turn for the worse. Iraq reiterated its claim on two Kuwaiti islands situated between Iraq and mainland Kuwait, Warbah and Bubiyan. These claims dated back to 1961 when the United Kingdom granted Kuwait its independence. At that time, Iraq asserted that Kuwait was an integral part of Iraq, having been part of the Ottoman province of Al-Basrah. However, the threat of a confrontation with British troops and military units from the Arab League (Egyptian, Saudi, Jordanian, and Sudanese) forced Iraq to back down.[2] The two islands were important to Baghdad because they control the estuary Khawr 'Abdallah, which at that time was the only access to the Persian Gulf.[3]

Saddam Husayn, leading Iraq to the status of a pariah nation in the region, began to threaten Iraq's neighbors in a series of public speeches. In addition to his earlier threats to burn Israel with chemical weapons, Saddam threatened unidentified action against Kuwait for that state's alleged illegal extraction of oil from the Al-Rumaylah oil field that straddles the Iraq-Kuwait border. These threats were being monitored closely in the West, especially by the U.S. Defense Department.

CENTCOM was concerned about Iraqi intentions toward Kuwait and about any potential threat to oil-rich Saudi Arabia, America's primary strategic interest in the area. For years, CENTCOM's primary focus had been on Iran. Following the overthrow of the shah in 1979 and establishment of an anti-American theocracy, the Defense Department formed the Rapid Deployment Joint Task Force (RDJTF, from which CENTCOM evolved) to focus on military operations in the area. The RDJTF developed a series of war plans to defend Iran, both with and without Iranian cooperation, from a Soviet thrust toward the warm waters of the Persian Gulf and the Indian Ocean. In the late 1980s, with the decline of the Soviet Union as a world power, CENTCOM planners began to reassess the threats to U.S. national interests in the area.

In 1989, following Iraq's unwillingness to demobilize its massive armed forces more rapidly and its relentless pursuit of weapons of mass destruction and more capable ballistic missiles, General Schwarzkopf informed senior Department of Defense officials that he intended to redirect CENTCOM planning efforts. He directed his staff to develop contingency plans to defend the Gulf Arab states, primarily Kuwait and Saudi Arabia, from an Iraqi invasion. Washington analysts did not believe Iraq was a threat to Iraq's Arab neighbors to the south. A year later,

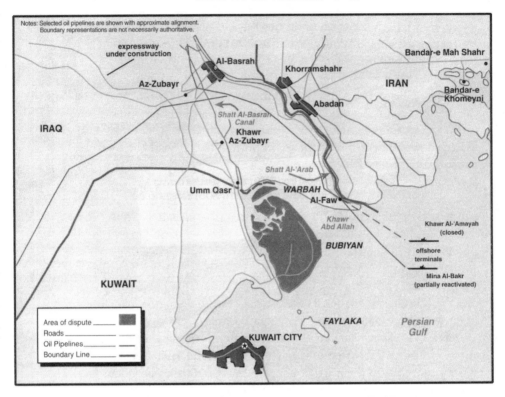

The Kuwaiti islands of Bubiyan and Warbah controlled Iraqi access to the Persian Gulf and were claimed by Iraq. *DOD*

CENTCOM was proven right in its analysis of the political situation in the area. By the time the Iraqi rhetoric reached its bellicose peak in the summer of 1990, CENTCOM was busily developing its plan to defend the Arabian Peninsula: Operations Plan 1002, or OPLAN 1002. Ironically, in July CENTCOM conducted Internal Look-90, a massive exercise (over six thousand participants) of its new plan, predicated on an Iraqi invasion of Kuwait and Saudi Arabia.

CENTCOM, unlike most other U.S. regional military commands, has its headquarters not within its area of responsibility but at MacDill Air Force Base in Tampa, Florida.[4] In 1990, with the exception of a small naval presence in the Gulf, there were no U.S. forces permanently deployed to the region. Prior to any significant military operation in the Persian Gulf, the CENTCOM staff would have to plan and coordinate the details of moving from garrison locations in the United States to the Middle East the entire force structure needed to execute a particular operation—a challenge for any logistics officer. With the exception of some small training deployments, the United States had never moved combat troops to the Arabian Peninsula before.

Convincing Arab leaders to accept American forces on their soil was problematic. There had to be a discernible threat to an Arab state before a leader such as the emir of Kuwait or the king of Saudi Arabia would ask for U.S. military assistance. In military planning parlance, this discernible threat is an "unambiguous warning."

To make their plan work, the CENTCOM staff needed thirty days of unambiguous warning prior to the onset of combat operations in the region. This thirty days would give the command enough time to convince Arab leaders that a deployment of American forces was required and would allow sufficient time to move enough force to protect the Saudi port facilities in the Gulf from being taken over in an Iraqi assault. Access to these modern ports would be critical to assembling enough combat power to eject the Iraqi forces that had entered Saudi Arabia.

This planning process caused great friction between the CENTCOM staff in Tampa and the national military staffs in Washington by mid to late 1989. CENTCOM's intelligence officers believed that they could provide the national and CENTCOM leadership with thirty days of unambiguous warning of an Iraqi attack into Kuwait or Saudi Arabia, based on the amount of time it would take Iraq to mass the necessary forces required to execute the assault. CENTCOM analysts postulated that to seize Kuwait effectively and mount a threat to Saudi Arabia, the Iraqis would need to deploy a force of at least ten divisions to the Iraq-Kuwait border. The analysts in Tampa were on the money. In August 1990, the Iraqis used just over eleven divisions to seize Kuwait and position a threatening force on the Saudi border.

Defense Intelligence Agency analysts took exception to the plan's presumption that U.S. forces could prevent Iraq from seizing Kuwait. The DIA had written an exhaustive study on Iraqi capabilities in 1989 that described how as few as five divisions could seize Kuwait before the U.S. could move enough forces to the region to stop such an attack.[5] The postulated attack plan was remarkably similar to the actual attack conducted a year later. DIA analysts felt that an unambiguous warning time of five to seven days was more realistic. CENTCOM and the DIA argued for months over the thirty-day figure. The argument was finally presented to General Schwarzkopf and the director of the DIA, Lt. Gen. Ed Soyster. Though the two had been personal friends for years, they could not reach agreement on the unambiguous warning time. In fact, the issue caused a lasting rift in their relationship.

Both the DIA and CENTCOM had overestimated. In the end, we had only three days of unambiguous warning of the attack into Kuwait. Even with the three days of warning, it was not until mere hours before the initial Iraqi assault into Kuwait that the emir asked for U.S. assistance, and it was not until four days later that the Saudi king authorized the initial deployment of American forces to the kingdom. By that time, now already 6 August, the Iraqis had eleven divisions (with over two thousand tanks) either present in or deploying to Kuwait and had positioned armor and mechanized infantry units along the Kuwaiti-Saudi border.

While harsh rhetoric had been spewing forth from Baghdad in July, the Iraqis launched a "charm offensive" in Arab capitals and Washington, D.C. The Iraqi military attaché had completed his three-year tour of duty in Washington and was due to return home. In mid-July, at his elegant Crystal City penthouse apartment overlooking Washington, Brig. Gen. Nabil Sa'id hosted a reception, which my wife and I attended as part of the DIA's representational contingent. At the reception, he introduced his replacement, who had flown in from Baghdad for a few days to meet Nabil's key contacts in both government and the private sector. Since the decline of official relations between Baghdad and Washington in general, and between the Iraqi Ministry of Defense and the Pentagon in particular, most of Nabil's work had shifted from military contacts to procuring equipment and technology for Iraq's advanced weapons programs. Always the consummate hosts, Nabil and his wife, Layla, represented their country in a favorable light, characterizing the harsh words from their government as a product of inter-Arab politics that was intended for domestic consumption. However, those of us who had spent a lot of time with Nabil sensed his discomfort with the situation.

During the following week, as the tone of the statements coming out of Baghdad had grown more bellicose, the Iraqi ambassador to the United States, Muhammad Al-Mash'at, hosted an uncharacteristically large celebration on the anniversary of Iraq's 17 July revolution. The reception, so large that it could not be held at the Iraqi embassy or ambassador's residence, took place at the Marriott Hotel in Crystal City (just outside Washington in Arlington, Virginia). Hundreds of diplomats and invited guests attended, including a large turnout from the local Iraqi and Iraqi-American community. U.S. government representation, reflecting the current crisis of words and threats in the Gulf, was limited.

There were no military officers present. I was selected to attend to represent the DIA but was told to wear civilian clothes rather than my air force uniform, which would have been customary on such an occasion. It was felt that the presence of someone senior to me would send too positive and supportive a signal to the Iraqis while they were involved in a war of words with the Gulf Arabs. Here as well, the ambassador attempted to portray the difficulties in the Gulf as matters between brother Arab states that, as such, would be resolved through Arab channels. Interestingly, Ambassador Al-Mash'at defected to Canada after the Iraqi invasion of Kuwait rather than return to Baghdad following the severance of relations between the United States and Iraq.

On that same day in 1990, 17 July, Saddam accused Kuwait and the United Arab Emirates of cheating on oil production quotas established by OPEC, thus lowering prices and reducing Iraq's income. It also accused Kuwait of slant drilling under the Kuwaiti border into Iraqi oil fields, in effect stealing Iraqi oil. At this time, Iraq needed all the income it could generate. Despite its massive foreign debt burden, it was still pouring money into its military programs. Iraq's defense budget in 1990 was 12.9 billion dollars, or about seven hundred dollars per citizen in a country where the average annual income was under two thousand dollars. Cash reserves had dwindled to enough for only three months of imports, and the inflation rate had soared to 40 percent.

The next day, 18 July, CENTCOM analysts reiterated their April warning to Washington of Iraqi antagonism toward Kuwait. By this time, U.S. intelligence had detected the initial movements of two Iraqi Republican Guard armored divisions from their garrison locations headed south. Given the sequence of events and the gravity of Iraq's financial situation, senior DIA Middle East specialists alerted the Joint Chiefs of Staff that Iraqi forces were deploying in a manner that suggested actual operations rather than exercise activity. By 21 July, combat elements of the two Republican Guard armor divisions were observed just north of the Kuwaiti border; however, the required communications, logistics, and air defense units that would be needed to support an attack into Kuwait were not present. A few days later these additional elements arrived in marshaling areas north of the Kuwaiti border, along with large numbers of artillery pieces and battlefield rocket launchers.

Reporting from intelligence assets in Kuwait indicated that the Iraqi embassy in Kuwait City had just been augmented by as many as three hundred new "diplomats," all in excellent physical condition and extremely active in moving around the city. The assessment was that a special-forces unit was conducting last-minute preattack reconnaissance of the city. CENTCOM and the DIA assumed WATCHCON III (increased threat to U.S. citizens, interests, or operating forces) on 21 July and WATCHCON II on 25 July. The DIA issued warnings that the situation between Iraq and Kuwait posed a significant threat to U.S. interests and assessed that Iraqi force levels were now sufficient to conduct operations against Kuwait with little or no warning. The DIA estimated that Iraqi forces could overrun all of Kuwait in five days.

It was against this backdrop that Brigadier Sa'id paid his final courtesy call on the leadership at the DIA. All foreign military attachés assigned to the United States are accredited to the director of the DIA. Part of that process is the presentation of credentials to the director at the beginning of the tour of duty and a final courtesy call on the director at the end of the tour. Given the buildup of Iraqi forces in a position that threatened a state friendly to the United States, the director and deputy director (both general officers) declined to meet with Nabil. He was met instead by the DIA chief of staff (a civilian employee), an undisguised slight. With the same reasoning that was used in regard to the Iraqi ambassador's anniversary reception, I was selected to escort Nabil to the meeting rather than have a more senior officer or DIA official participate.

At the meeting, the acting DIA chief of staff bluntly expressed regret that Nabil's country had chosen to mass its forces on the border of a neighboring country, to issue intimidating statements, and to threaten peace in the region. Nabil had hoped to depart the United States on good terms—after all, he had been a key player in developing the close and successful relationship between the Department of Defense and the Iraqi military two years earlier. He was a professional military officer carrying out his orders, not a political decision-maker in Baghdad.

After listening to the chief of staff voice his opinion on Iraq's current misdeeds in the region, Nabil stood, thanked the official for his time, offered his hand, and left. As I escorted him to the exit, we had a chance to talk for a few minutes. He said he was happy to be going home; his father was in poor health, and it was time for his children to get to know their homeland. He said that he was concerned about the current situation and hoped it would be resolved peacefully but that, in his opinion, matters did not portend well. I asked if his replacement was due back in Washington anytime soon. He shook his head and said it was not likely, given the bitterness of the rhetoric on both sides of the crisis. I saluted what I considered to be a fellow professional military officer, shook his hand, and wished him the best. He had served his nation and uniform well, and he was saddened to depart under the cloud of potential conflict.

On 25 July, Ambassador Glaspie met with Saddam Husayn in Baghdad at the Iraqi leader's "invitation," which was actually more of a summons. This was her first private meeting with Saddam—the Iraqi dictator did not like Glaspie. Saddam told the ambassador that he had just had a telephone conversation with Egyptian president Husni Mubarak, during which he agreed to solve the Kuwaiti problem through negotiations. Mubarak later conceded that Saddam had lied to him and that the Iraqi dictator had probably already made the decision to invade Kuwait.

That same day in Washington the director of Central Intelligence, William Webster, briefed President Bush that the intelligence community believed an Iraqi attack into Kuwait was possible, given the deployment of Iraqi forces on the Kuwaiti border. The analysis was shared with Egypt's President Mubarak, Jordan's King Hussein, Saudi Arabia's King Fahd, and the emir of Kuwait. All four Arab leaders, including the emir, reassured Bush that they knew Saddam Husayn better than American intelligence analysts and that while the Iraqi leader was trying to intimidate Kuwait, an attack on a fellow Arab state was out of the question. The Arabs hoped the situation could be resolved at the next meeting of OPEC, scheduled for 28 July in Jiddah, Saudi Arabia. At that meeting, Iraq and Kuwait agreed to meet again on 31 July, using the good offices of the king of Saudi Arabia.

On 27 July, my office advised the Kuwaiti ambassador to the United States, Sheikh Nasir Al-Sabah, that we believed—barring a change in Kuwait's position toward Baghdad's demands—Iraq would invade Kuwait. Although some analysts preferred to soften that assessment,

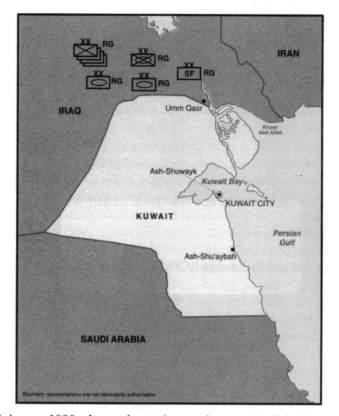

By 1 August 1990, almost the entire combat power of the Republican Guard Forces Command was poised on the Kuwaiti border. *DOD*

over the next few days we sent several memoranda to the director of the DIA and the director of intelligence for the Joint Chiefs, concluding that unless there was some unforeseen change in the situation, Iraqi forces would cross the border into Kuwait within the next forty-eight hours. By this time, Iraq had amassed eight Republican Guard divisions, including three heavy (armored or mechanized infantry) divisions, north of the Kuwaiti border.

At the 31 July meeting in Jiddah, deputy chairman of Iraq's Revolutionary Command Council Izzat Ibrahim Al-Duri continued to spout the same harsh, if not harsher, rhetoric of the past weeks. Hopes for a diplomatic solution to the crisis evaporated. The failure of this meeting and the movement of additional Iraqi artillery units to the Kuwaiti border on 1 August (bringing the number of Iraqi troops to over a hundred and forty thousand) prompted both DIA and CENTCOM watch centers to declare WATCHCON I—the highest watch condition, a warning of an imminent threat to U.S. national interests in the clear and immediate possibility of an invasion. Yet despite all these indications and warnings from the intelligence community, no U.S. forces had been alerted, nor had any logistics preparations been made to support a potential deployment of forces to the region.

That same afternoon, I had lunch with two officials from the Israeli embassy. As was to be expected, the crisis in the Gulf was the only topic of conversation—Israel remained wary of Iraq's threats and its arsenal of chemical weapons and ballistic missiles. We advised the Israeli officers that we expected an Iraqi invasion of Kuwait at any time, as early as that evening.

On 2 August, at 1:00 A.M. Kuwait time, the three Iraqi Republican Guard heavy divisions moved across the Kuwaiti border. They were supported by combat aircraft and a helicopter-borne special forces air assault on Kuwait City. By 5:30 A.M. the heavy divisions had reached the outskirts of Kuwait City. The city fell by early evening, and Iraqi tanks moved to occupy positions south of the capital. Armored columns continued to move toward the Saudi border. As these units were consolidating their hold on Kuwait, at least four additional armor and mechanized infantry divisions began to move out of their home garrisons in Iraq and head south for Kuwait. The attack had been executed flawlessly, and additional units were pouring into the operations area. To analysts at CENT-COM headquarters and in various watch centers in and around Washington, it appeared that the follow-on forces would replace the Republican Guard units that had conducted the invasion. The big question was where the Republican Guard divisions were headed—back north to Iraq or south into Saudi Arabia.

It was unclear what Saddam's immediate intentions were. Ideally, intelligence analysts deal with both enemy intentions and capabilities. We were fairly confident in our knowledge of Iraq's military capabilities because we had closely observed Iraqi performance against the Iranians for almost eight years. Also, Iraq's invasion of Kuwait closely matched the DIA scenario written a year earlier. However, with no reliable intelligence on Saddam's intentions, analysts looked for patterns

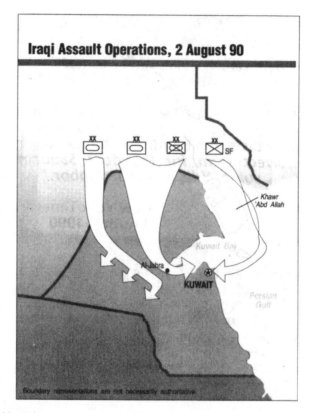

Iraqi Assault Operations, 2 August 90

The Iraqi invasion was executed with a main attack by an armored and mechanized infantry division, supported by an additional armored division to the west and a heliborne special forces division attack on Kuwait City. *DOD*

of activity that had been observed before. The situation on the ground resembled classic Iraqi offensive doctrine. Republican Guard forces had completed their attack into Kuwait and moved all the way to the Saudi border. The regular army units following them were in the process of replacing the Republican Guard on the Saudi border. As the Iraqis had done in the offensives of 1988, the regular forces could be moving into forward positions opposite enemy forces and preparing the way for Republican Guard forces to pass through to attack into Saudi Arabia. Given the seriousness of the situation, the analysts opted for the "worst case" and assessed that sufficient Iraqi forces were in place to launch an attack into Saudi Arabia with little or no warning.

They also assessed that the Iraqi forces were capable of easily overwhelming Saudi defenses and seizing the oil-rich Eastern Province and the kingdom's major Gulf ports. If the assault were successful, Saddam would not only gain control over 40 percent of the world's proven oil reserves and much of the world's oil refining capability but also close off the most likely debarkation points for any foreign forces entering Saudi Arabia.

U.S. policy makers wrestled with the effects of the invasion and total takeover of Kuwait. Options were discussed and plans reviewed as analysts tried to discern Saddam's intentions. Saddam now had a formidable force positioned just north of Saudi Arabia's major oil-producing region, facing vastly outnumbered and outgunned Saudi ground force and National Guard units. On 5 August, President Bush sent Secretary of Defense Dick Cheney and CENTCOM commander in chief General Schwarzkopf to Saudi Arabia to consult with King Fahd. The secretary and General Schwarzkopf outlined the military situation for the Saudi monarch.

Iraqi forces, with little or no warning, could launch an attack south into Saudi Arabia and seize the kingdom's primary oil fields, adding control of another 20 percent of the world's proven oil reserves, in addition to the 20 percent Saddam now controlled in Iraq and Kuwait. Militarily, moreover, this thrust would close off Saudi Arabia's modern and efficient port facilities—assets that would be essential if American forces were to deploy to defend the area. Saddam's intentions remained unclear.

By 6 August, the Iraqis had major elements of at least eleven combat divisions in Kuwait. Faced with the presence of an overwhelming Iraqi military force on the Saudi border, the king opted to ask for American forces to help defend the kingdom. On 7 August, President Bush ordered the deployment of U.S. air and ground forces to Saudi Arabia, augmenting U.S. Navy ships already moving to the region. Operation Desert Shield had begun.

Within hours, the 1st Tactical Fighter Wing's F-15 Eagle fighter aircraft and the alert brigade of the 82d Airborne Division were airborne and en route to Saudi Arabia. "Pre-po" ships—ships loaded with U.S. Marine Corps combat materiel and pre-positioned (hence the name) in various ports around the world—set sail from Diego Garcia in the

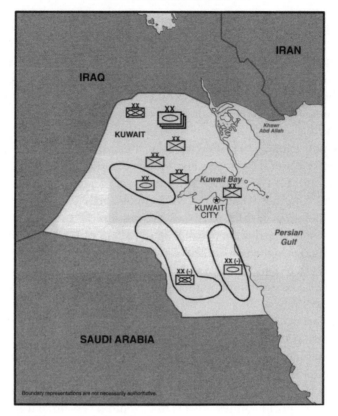

By 6 August 1990, additional armored and mechanized units were entering Kuwait, freeing up for further action, possibly against Saudi Arabia, the Republican Guard troops who had conducted the invasion. *DOD*

Indian Ocean, bound for the Persian Gulf. A massive military logistics machine began the tightly choreographed movement of hundreds of thousands of personnel, vehicles, aircraft, ships, and supplies halfway around the world.

With the deployment of U.S. forces to the region, determining Saddam's intentions regarding Saudi Arabia took on new urgency.[6] Although a small number of American troops had arrived in the kingdom and thousands more were on the way, Iraqi forces still held the upper hand. In hindsight, Saddam missed his window of opportunity to take Saudi Arabia's eastern oil fields. Every day he waited, that window closed a bit more as additional U.S. forces poured into Saudi Arabia.

In the Joint Chiefs war-gaming center in the basement of the Pentagon, every conceivable scenario was being run through a bank of computers to determine what force mix would be required to stop Iraqi movements into Saudi Arabia and whether levels of U.S. forces at a particular time would be sufficient to repel the attack. Despite the overwhelming relative strength of the Iraqi force—tanks, artillery, and troops—the computer results consistently showed that American air power available soon after initial deployments—which included air force, navy, and army aircraft—would be sufficient to stop Iraqi units before they could reach the main Saudi ports at Damman and Dhahran.

Those of us who had served in Iraq and had seen Iraqi capabilities were skeptical. Even after adjustments were made to the computer models to dilute the capabilities of the American aircraft, the results were always the same. The computer simulations, based on years of statistical research, were probably correct, but Schwarzkopf, not a strong believer in air power, never considered Saddam's window of opportunity actually closed until the arrival of the 24th Mechanized Infantry Division in October.

Later, after the battle of Al-Khafji in late January 1991, when U.S. air power devastated Iraqi armored columns moving south to reinforce units engaged in battle, it became clear that the computer simulations had been accurate. As vast numbers of men and equipment poured into the desert on both sides of the Saudi border, armed conflict appeared inevitable.

4

Riyadh

THE COALITION

Shortly after the CENTCOM headquarters staff deployed to Saudi Arabia in August, General Schwarzkopf advised his director of intelligence, Brig. Gen. Jack Leide, that he wanted a military officer to serve as his Arabic interpreter rather than a civilian offered by the State Department. Leide—an airborne ranger and Vietnam combat veteran who had made a name for himself while serving as the U.S. defense attaché in China during the Tienanmen Square crisis—asked his deputy, air force colonel Karl Polifka, to locate an Arabic-speaking military officer, preferably with on-the-ground experience in Iraq.

Polifka was familiar with the military cooperation efforts in 1988 and with the short-term relationship that had existed between the Iraqi military and the Defense Department. From his previous assignments in air force intelligence, he was also aware of my experiences in Baghdad and my associated travels in Iraq and the region. He recommended to the intelligence director that the DIA be requested to make me available to serve as the interpreter for the CENTCOM commander in chief. There was no doubt as to the answer. Soon after American forces were ordered to the region, the word went out from the chairman of the Joint Chiefs of Staff, Gen. Colin Powell, that all CENTCOM requests for assistance were to be treated as priority one.

The DIA, anxious to provide support to the effort, readily agreed to the CENTCOM request for my services. Orders assigning me to temporary duty at "CENTCOM Forward" in Riyadh, a process normally requiring several days, were published in hours. Desert camouflage uniforms and special equipment (weapon, gas mask, web belt, and so forth) were put into duffel bags and flown on the CENTCOM courier flight to Andrews AFB, Maryland, the next day. I was handed airline tickets for a Pan American Airways flight to Riyadh leaving in two days. It appeared that I might again see Baghdad and my old friends, although this time in much different circumstances.

I departed Washington's Dulles Airport the beginning of September. My wife, herself an air force officer, took me to the airport and, like so many times before, saw me off on a trip to the Middle East. This time was different, though, and we both knew it. There was an air of tension at the airport. All around were signs of the movement of American troops and materiel to the Middle East—charter flights and a lot of people in uniform, many carrying their weapons. Although my earlier trips to the region had involved some element of personal risk, this time I had no idea when or—should things go really badly—if I would be coming home.

I arrived in Riyadh in the late afternoon. I had not been in the Saudi capital for seven years, and the city had grown since then. The old airport I remembered from a decade ago was now a Saudi air base, and the new airport was the epitome of the financial excess we had come to call "Saudi gaudy." The sleepy, dusty Arab city I remembered was now a thriving business and economic hub. The Saudis, having acquired wealth beyond their wildest expectations, had come to appreciate the things that money could buy—and they bought a lot of them.

As I prepared to go through Saudi customs, I remembered the zeal with which the inspectors had sought out even the slightest affront to Wahabbi Islam, the ultraconservative style of Islam practiced by the ruling Sa'ud family. However, I was shocked by the friendly, almost warm, reception I was given when I produced my official passport and said in Arabic to the inspector, "Good afternoon, I'm with the United States Air Force." I was astonished that several of the idle inspectors made a point to come over and welcome me to Saudi Arabia and rush me through customs. Anybody who has visited Saudi Arabia either before or after Desert Shield and Desert Storm can understand my surprise.

Although the Saudis, both military personnel and civilians, welcomed the arriving American forces with open arms, there were many Americans at our embassy who seemed to resent our presence. Perhaps they regarded the deployment of U.S. forces as an indication that they, the diplomats, had failed and it was now time to resort to the military option—I don't know. I remember an incident at the U.S. commissary when a mid-level State Department employee loudly complained that the troops were buying all the items and should be prohibited from shopping in the facility—one owned and operated by the Department of Defense primarily for personnel assigned to the U.S. Military Training Mission in Saudi Arabia. I was impressed with the polite, almost deferential manner with which the target of his outburst, a group of young U.S. Army soldiers—tough paratroopers—defused the situation.

Upon arrival, I was billeted at the Hyatt Regency Hotel, directly across the street from the Saudi Ministry of Defense and Aviation (MODA). (I was later moved to what was commonly known as the Lockheed compound, which had been leased by the Lockheed company but was vacated when the company's dependents were evacuated from the kingdom at the start of the crisis.) While life in the well-appointed hotel was deceptively calm, the almost continuous roar overhead from U.S. Air Force heavy airlift jets and chartered airliners used as troop ferries making their approach to Riyadh Air Base was a constant reminder of the situation.

CENTCOM had established its forward headquarters in the two-story bunker a hundred feet beneath the MODA building. Since General Schwarzkopf did not require an interpreter on a full-time basis, my initial duties were in the directorate of intelligence, working with the staff to develop and institutionalize cooperative relationships with the Saudis and other members of the coalition. Things were still in the formative stages, but I was often called upon to provide current situation briefings in Arabic to senior Saudi officers, mostly repeating what was being briefed to the senior U.S. staff in English earlier in the day.

One of the officers whom I briefed regularly was Maj. Gen. Yusif Madani, the deputy chief of staff for operations and plans. A graduate of numerous U.S. military command and staff schools, General Madani understood the magnitude of the Iraqi threat as well as the challenge of moving the vast quantities of personnel and equipment from the United States to Saudi Arabia. Unlike other Saudi officers who lacked his experience, he appreciated the size and doctrinal differences between the U.S. and Saudi militaries. In 1990, the Saudis' largest organized military unit was the brigade (seventy-five hundred men), and most training and exercises were conducted at the reinforced battalion (two thousand men) level. To counter the Iraqi threat, the coalition, overwhelmingly dominated by American troops, was putting into place the command and control mechanisms that would eventually direct the operations of the equivalent of five corps (over five hundred thousand troops) in combat. Movements on this scale had not been attempted since World War II.

Despite the fact that the Saudis knew they faced a real threat to their survival as an independent kingdom, they remained wary of the influx of massive numbers of mostly non-Muslim troops onto what they consider holy ground. Islam's two holiest cities, Mecca (Al-Makkah Al-Mukaramah) and Medina (Al-Madinah Al-Munawirah) are located in the western part of the kingdom. The ruling family of Saudi Arabia, the house of Sa'ud, derives its legitimacy and social contract from its status as protector of the faith. Although the ruler of Saudi Arabia is normally referred to as King Fahd, his official title is "Custodian of the Two Holy Sites." Inscribed on every piece of official stationery of the Kingdom of Saudi Arabia are the words "In the Name of God the Merciful, the Compassionate." The Shari'a, Islamic law, is the law of the land. The Saudi national flag bears no emblem or adornment other than a sword and the words "There is no God but God, and Muhammad is the Messenger of God."

There was no precedent for the Saudis to follow in this crisis situation. This was the first time foreign forces had been invited to the kingdom. On one hand, the Saudi government was faced with the task of allowing hundreds of thousands of foreigners, mostly Christians, into the kingdom while adhering to the social contract of an Islamic state. On the other hand, CENTCOM military planners were forced to address Saudi concerns that were not the usual issues to arise during the deployment of military forces. Saudi military mullahs, equivalent to chaplains in the U.S. military but with much greater influence, demanded that special arrangements be made not only to segregate the troops by religion but also to separate the by-products their presence itself created. For example, the Saudis initially advised that all sewage generated by American camps and installations would have to be removed from Saudi Arabia. It could not be allowed to contaminate Saudi soil. Blood supplies for military hospitals would have to kept separate so that Christian and Muslim blood was never allowed to mix. Christian casualties could not be buried in Saudi Arabia. Though all these demands were taken to the most senior levels, often all the way to King Fahd himself, they were resolved quickly when saner heads prevailed.

However, one sticking point did remain: church services. American troops sent off to war have always been accompanied by their chaplains, be they Catholic, Protestant, Jewish, or Muslim. Freedom of religion is a basic tenet of the United States. No American leader could send U.S. troops overseas and tell them they could not practice their religion of choice. Yet because of their religious laws, the Saudis would not allow Christian and Jewish services on their soil. The answer was for chaplains on military facilities to hold "morale calls." As long as the Saudis were not faced with notifications of church services, they turned a blind eye to these observances—which were labeled "morale call-C" for Catholic, "morale call-P" for Protestant, and "morale call-J" for Jewish. It was fairly evident to everyone what was going on, but it provided the respective leaderships deniability. The Saudis, for their part, undertook not-too-subtle attempts to spread Islam among U.S. forces, expending a fair amount of money on literature and gifts to potential converts, with some limited success.[1]

As Christmas approached, many American troops had been in Saudi Arabia for four months. Christmas is always a tough time emotionally for service members away from their homes and families. To make it easier, many troops created makeshift Christmas trees, some quite ingenious. However, Saudi officers regarded these holiday decorations as symbols of Christianity and demanded that they be removed. Most were taken down, but a few subtle representations remained, largely out of a sense of rebellion and resentment. Many troops grumbled that if American troops could deploy to Saudi Arabia to defend the kingdom, they should have the right to display Christmas decorations. Others expressed disappointment that senior American military and political officials did not take a tougher stand with the Saudis over this issue.

Another big issue tied to Saudi law was alcohol—Islam forbids the drinking of alcohol. In order to prevent any problems from the use of alcohol by American troops, General Schwarzkopf simply forbade members of the U.S. armed forces in Saudi Arabia to drink. It was the grossly unpopular "General Order Number One." Yet many Saudi officers did drink alcohol in private. American officers who were invited to visit their Saudi counterparts in their homes were routinely offered alcoholic beverages, and the Saudi officers themselves exhibited no reluctance to drink despite the U.S. officers' refusals. There was, and had been for years, a burgeoning black market in alcohol reminiscent of Prohibition in the United States in the 1920s. The going price for a bottle of Johnny Walker Black Label Scotch was around a hundred dollars, and the Saudis were willing to pay for it.

One of the most complex problems facing all of the nations sending troops to participate in the coalition against Iraq was the command and control structure: who was to command whose troops. Almost all nations were reluctant to place their military forces under the command of foreign officers. Some nations did not have the legal mechanism to place their forces under foreign command, while others were hesitant to do so because of national pride. As the largest provider of forces, the United States, in the person of General Schwarzkopf, was assumed to play the dominant leadership role. The Saudis, as the host nation, believed that they should have, if not the dominant position, a prominent one.

The Saudis were adamant in demanding a senior leadership position, but the United States never seriously considered placing its troops under Saudi command. To satisfy the requirements of all the governments involved, therefore, a parallel command structure was established. It was confusing at first, but eventually the bugs were worked out. Only a few Western nations provided combat forces, although many nations provided support forces, such as medical units, transportation units, and airlift. In addition to those from the United States, combat ground units and aircraft from the United Kingdom and France, and combat aircraft from Canada and Italy, were present. It was originally thought that these units would fight under American command, but the French balked and were placed in an associate position with the Saudis. This arrangement lasted until Desert Storm, when the French agreed to allow their forces to fight attached to, and under the command of, the XVIII Airborne Corps. The British 7th Armoured Brigade, the lineal "Desert Rats" of World War II fame, became an integral part of CENTCOM's ground component. Other national prerogatives also had to be addressed, such as Canada's prohibition of its aircraft entering Iraqi or Kuwaiti airspace.

The Saudis had an equal (on paper) command structure for the Arab and Muslim combat forces sent to Saudi Arabia as part of the coalition. This was called the Joint Forces Command (JFC), under Saudi

Air Defense Force chief Lt. Gen. (Prince) Khalid bin Sultan bin 'Abd Al-'Aziz. There was little reluctance for the Arab and Muslim countries to place their forces into this command structure. The Gulf Cooperation Council member countries had long-established military relationships, with Saudi Arabia in the de facto leadership role. The Egyptians and Syrians formed a three-division corps under Egyptian command. This and other national units became part of the Saudi command as well.

For the duration of the national emergency facing the kingdom, the Saudi Arabian National Guard (SANG) was placed under temporary JFC operational control. The SANG is personally commanded by Crown Prince 'Abdallah bin 'Abd Al-'Aziz and is not a part of the Ministry of Defense and Aviation. Although the Saudis claim that SANG is a cultural and military force paralleling the U.S. National Guard, it is today an independent regime-protection paramilitary force to counterbalance the power of the armed forces, which in the Middle East are always considered potential sources of rebellion.[2] The temporary subordination of the SANG to the regular military revealed the seriousness with which the Saudis viewed the situation following Iraq's invasion and occupation of Kuwait.

The JFC commander, Prince Khalid bin Sultan, was a product of his environment. Younger than many of the senior officers assigned to his JFC staff, he appeared to be a bit unsure of himself in military matters, though not in being a prince. Although comfortable with the trappings of wealth and deference that are part of being a member of the immediate Saudi royal family, he appeared uneasy when discussing military strategy with a soldier the likes of General Schwarzkopf.

After the end of Desert Storm, Khalid wrote a book called *Desert Warrior*, in which he describes his experiences as the commander of JFC. The book appears to be an attempt to justify his selection as the JFC commander ahead of other qualified, more experienced officers—downplaying the fact that he is the son of Minister of Defense and Aviation Prince Sultan bin 'Abd Al-'Aziz and the nephew of King Fahd.[3] Khalid also tries to create the impression that he held the coalition together in the face of American efforts to dominate military decisions. Although he played a role in maintaining the coalition—Khalid has an excellent command of the English language and is comfortable working with Westerners—the idea that JFC and CENTCOM were equal commands is nonsense.

To bridge the gap between the two parallel command structures, the Coalition Coordination, Communications, and Integration Center, or C3IC, was set up adjacent to the CENTCOM command post in the bunker under the MODA building. In reality, the C3IC served as the Saudi command post. U.S. and French officers were assigned to the C3IC as liaison officers. Because of my language capabilities, when not interpreting for the command section, I spent most of my time in the C3IC as a liaison between Saudi commanders and the CENTCOM director of intelligence.

Working with Saudi counterparts provided me an excellent education in the Saudi culture. Although I had spent a fair amount of time in the Middle East and a little time in Saudi Arabia, I had not learned that much about the Saudis. I became acquainted with several Saudi captains, majors, and lieutenant colonels in the land force, navy, and air force. For the most part they were friendly toward the Americans and appreciated the fact that the United States was willing to assist in the defense of the kingdom. Nevertheless, they were wary of what American intentions might be after the end of the crisis. During the hours we spent together in the C3IC, we discussed all facets of life in both countries. Many of the Saudis had attended college or military training schools in the United States.

In preparation for deployment to the area, many of the American troops attempted to read background material and histories of Saudi Arabia. The history of Saudi Arabia as a kingdom is fairly short: the present king is a son of the founder of the kingdom. However, the land itself is the home of ancient cultures and one of the world's major religions. While the Saudis were fairly conversant in the history of Islam and its spread throughout the Middle East, North Africa, South Asia, and parts of Europe, they were surprisingly unaware of the history of their own kingdom. Some of the most popular and well-written histories of the kingdom were banned. Accurate information that portrayed anything derogatory about members of the royal family was simply not available to the population. Accounts that were available did not cover the royal family in detail. We found that most of the U.S. Middle East foreign area officers and specialists knew far more about the Saudi government than most Saudi military officers knew—and certainly more about the royal family. Most of the Saudi officers were uncomfortable when talking about the royal family, fearing they might be called to account for discussing with foreigners what is considered a sensitive subject.

Most of the Americans had heard of the Saudi justice system, most notably the practice of public beheadings. The Saudis were proud of their system and were eager to show it to visitors. In downtown Riyadh, outside the Ministry of Justice, is a large parking lot. On Fridays, the Muslim holy day, justice is meted out here. Crowds gather as murderers and rapists are beheaded. Executions are filmed for broadcast on that day's news shows. Adulterers are stoned in the modern way: a judge throws the ritual first stone, and then a dump truck is used to bury the convicted person under a load of rocks. And although hands are still cut off as punishment for theft, the procedure is done in a hospital.

Since there were a large number of American military women serving in the kingdom, Saudi attitudes toward women were always a hot topic. I engaged one of my counterparts, a Royal Saudi Air Force major who was a graduate of Oregon State University. His wife had accompanied him during his four years of study in the States. I asked him if she had obtained a driver's license in America and had driven a car. He replied that they both drove while he was in school. I asked if she missed having the right to drive now that they were back in Saudi Arabia. He replied that of course she did not. Curious, I asked why she was content to give up the right to drive. He countered that she did not need to drive, for he had provided her a chauffeur. This seemed like a valid point. When I asked if she too had attended college in the States, he replied that she had. When I asked if she worked here in the kingdom, he replied that she did not. I asked why not, and he replied that she did not want to. I asked if he had ever asked her if she wanted to work. He replied, "Why ask? I know the answer." It was impossible to break the circle.

Saudi attitudes toward women caused problems for the leadership as well. Laws forbidding women to drive had to be modified for American servicewomen. To their credit, U.S. commanders insisted that women were an integral part of their military units and had to be permitted to perform their assigned duties, including driving vehicles, for the units to be effective. Of course, in a society where any and all decisions had to be made at the highest levels, many of these issues were taken to the king. It was decreed that U.S. military women could operate only military vehicles—and only when dressed in military attire. The decree read literally that "U.S. female military personnel in uniform are not women when driving military vehicles." When I translated the order, I rendered it in a more politically palatable form: "U.S. military women may drive military vehicles while in uniform." In a similar vein, Saudi air base commanders insisted that women working on the hot, sunny flight line wear their long-sleeved desert camouflage jackets; males, under these same conditions, were allowed to remove their jackets and work in T-shirts. Many U.S. Air Force personnel felt they had been let down by their leadership when it appeared that no one was willing to confront the Saudi officers over what was a minor issue but a major irritant.

Saudi women are not permitted to be in public alone or to appear without being fully veiled. In Riyadh, the center of the very conservative Wahabbi Islam sect, the rules are vigorously enforced by a group of zealots called *mutawa'in*. These self-appointed religious police patrol the city streets and markets with thin camel whips and strike the back of the legs of women who offend their sense of morality or decency. They also enforce shop and restaurant closings during calls to prayer. Western women are not required to be fully veiled, but conservative clothing is advised. For the most part, American servicewomen wore thin black robes in an attempt to avoid offending their Saudi hosts. Occasionally a particularly aggressive mutawa' would harass an American servicewoman. Since I could speak the language, I was often asked to escort visiting senior officers and civilians to the souks downtown.

Several of the women in my housing compound, reluctant to go out without male escorts, asked if I would take a group downtown. One of the women was an air force captain with long blonde hair. Although she was properly attired in a black robe covering her from shoulders to well below her knees, her blonde hair was a beacon for attention by the Saudi males in the souk. Almost immediately after arriving, I noticed a mutawa' armed with a camel whip watching us closely. He continued to follow us, getting slowly closer. Figuring that this situation had the potential to get out of hand, I walked over to him and greeted him politely in Arabic. He instantly responded, "Your wife's hair—it is inflammatory. She is exciting the men!"

I saw a trap in the making. I could not claim that the captain was not my wife. Single women are not permitted to be in public with men, and married women must always be accompanied by their husbands or servants. Although we were not sure how this applied to the Desert Shield forces, the mutawa' obviously was under the impression that it did apply. Not wanting to see the Saudi strike the captain, and not sure how much damage she might wreak in return, I said that I was very sorry, that sometimes my wife was disobedient and I had not noticed how her hair appeared. I said that I was anxious to get her home to discipline her. He nodded, and we left. I thought it best not to relay the exact translation to the captain, again not sure of how much damage she might wreak.

American servicewomen assigned to duty in the kingdom performed admirably under conditions even more difficult than those for the men. Women had to put up with the additional restrictions—the clothing requirements, the difficulty in moving around the city without driving cars or using public transportation—and for the most part, they did not complain. The Saudis in the headquarters tended to ignore the military women, although not necessarily out of disrespect or arrogance. I think they just never learned how to speak to adult women except those in their immediate families.

Saudi treatment of women was puzzling to many of the American troops deployed to the kingdom. Most had never been exposed to a society so different from their own, and most arrived believing that because of the strict Islamic customs, there would be no social contact between the American servicemen and Saudi women. Rumors and stories, largely untrue, soon began to circulate among the Americans concerning Saudi dating customs. One actual custom, however, did surprise us—a rather unique practice that obviously grew out of the rigid Saudi standards of public conduct between the sexes.

While sitting on a bench in the mall area of one of Riyadh's modern shopping complexes, several of us observed occasional groups of young Saudi women, all appropriately clothed in black from head to foot, walking from the stores to their cars, usually with a uniformed driver as a chaperone. Sometimes, one of the young ladies would drop something on the floor near one of us. Initially it appeared that they had either unknowingly dropped a piece of paper or were just littering, which was not uncommon. However, the pieces of paper turned out to be business cards with first names and cellular telephone numbers printed on them.

When I asked a Saudi officer at work the next day what this all meant, he explained that this was a modern Saudi dating ritual. A young lady would drop the card near a young man she was interested in, a contact was made via cellular phone, and a discreet rendezvous arranged, usually at great risk. The officer then asked if I had noticed that young Saudi men usually drove around the malls with the front passenger window halfway down, despite the intense desert heat. I said that I had but had not attached any particular meaning to it. He explained that this was to provide a place for the young ladies to throw their cards. After hearing the explanation, I did notice that the mutawa'in were on the lookout for cars cruising the malls with the front passenger window rolled down.

As we grew closer to what probably would be a war with the Iraqis, the mood of the Saudis was fascinating to watch. Many of the officers came from wealthy families and had never thought about a threat to their status and fortunes.[4] As tensions increased, rhetoric grew more bellicose. Thousands of troops with the world's most sophisticated and lethal weaponry poured into the region, and some Saudi officers began looking for a safety net, a way out. For example, working in the C3IC, I had become close to several of the Saudi officers—they were intrigued with any American or Westerner who had mastered their language. One of the senior officers, a Royal Saudi Air Defense Force brigadier, approached me quietly and asked if we could speak in private.

Once alone, he asked me if it were true that persons born in the United States were automatically American citizens. I said that I believed that to be true in most cases. He said that while a young officer, he had been trained at the U.S. Army Air Defense Artillery School at Fort Bliss, located outside El Paso, Texas. While there, his wife had given birth to their daughter at the military hospital. He asked if his daughter was a U.S. citizen or was qualified to claim U.S. citizenship. Not being an immigration lawyer, I told him I would ask someone at the consular section of the embassy downtown. A month later, I took great pleasure in presenting him his daughter's American passport. I found it telling that when there was a threat to his country, he wished to explore his daughter's American citizenship status.

THE INTELLIGENCE LASH-UP

Working with our Saudi counterparts revealed differences in doctrine and methodology, including those in the intelligence apparatus of each nation. Since I was working in the C3IC as a liaison between the Saudi general staff and the CENTCOM director of intelligence, I was able to understand why our intelligence relationship was strained. We could never get information from the Saudis in a timely manner, and what we got was fragmented and contradictory. The problem was the difference in our two systems.

In the U.S. intelligence community, information is collected through a variety of means. We are very fortunate to have access to technology that provides satellites for this purpose, in addition to electronic sensors carried aboard ships and aircraft and at ground stations throughout the world. These technical collectors are complemented by a worldwide human intelligence system operated by both the Central Intelligence Agency and the Department of Defense. Intelligence is collected in response to requirements generated by policy makers and military commanders based on what information they need to have to accomplish their missions—anything from trade negotiations to the order of battle of a potential enemy.

Regardless of the method of collection, the data are considered "raw" and unevaluated and are passed to analytical centers in Washington and to intelligence staffs at the various military commands. Only after the information is analyzed, evaluated, and combined with other available raw information and research is it considered finished intelligence—the product that represents the assessment of the intelligence community and that is used by policy and decision makers. It is that analytical and evaluation process that distinguishes our system from the Saudi system.

Saudi intelligence collection is based almost entirely on human intelligence, with the exception of some tactical electronic intercept and aerial reconnaissance platforms operated by the Royal Saudi Air Force. There are various organizations that collect intelligence, but no coherent community exists for such. In almost all cases, the focus of the intelligence collection is to develop information on threats to the ruling family. Much of it is focused on internal security, and much of it is collected domestically. Little if any collection is geared toward developing intelligence on foreign military capabilities and intentions.

However, the major difference between the Saudi and American systems is the information flow. Raw information collected by Saudi intelligence officers in the field is sent directly to the head of the particular intelligence agency, bypassing any intermediate analysis element that would attempt to verify the information or at least to make a judgment call on the reliability of the source of the information. For example, a Saudi General Intelligence Directorate (GID) officer serving in Europe will report information to the head of the directorate rather than to a GID analytical cell. Since the sources are not tested and checked to determine reliability, and no analysis is applied to the information, the report is regarded as fact unless it can be proven to be inaccurate. There is the potential that policy decisions will be made on uncorroborated, raw data that have not been reviewed by analysts with access to multiple sources of information.

As we began to work with Saudi military intelligence, we often found ourselves in the position of having to refute baseless claims by Saudi agents throughout the region. Most notably, these dealt with alleged Iraqi missile and air threats against the kingdom, with the highest focus on threats against the king or his palaces. There were numerous incredible reports of Iraqi missiles and aircraft being moved undetected into Yemen or Sudan, where they posed a threat to the king, then in residence at his summer palace in Saudi Arabia's west-coast city of Jiddah. I think we must have utilized every collection asset against Yemen and the Sudan to prove that there were no Iraqi aircraft or missiles present. Yet each time such a report came in, no Saudi analysis was applied—there was merely an official memorandum from either the director of military intelligence or the head of GID, or sometimes General Khalid, requesting that we attempt to confirm or deny the report. The Saudis would not accept our analytical judgment that the information was too incredible. Usually they were not satisfied until we produced a full-blown intelligence report that showed empty airfields or unoccupied positions in specific locations.

Despite these incredible threat reports, King Fahd remained in Jiddah throughout almost the entire period of operations Desert Shield and Desert Storm, coming to Riyadh only occasionally. This was in marked contrast to his normal practice of spending the entire winter in Riyadh. Jiddah was out of range of any known or suspected Iraqi missile systems fired from Iraqi territory. There were rumors that the king remained in Jiddah because a soothsayer had warned that his death would occur in Riyadh.

As with any military deployment since Vietnam, the three major intelligence agencies sent teams to the area to support the combatant commander. Two of these national agencies are part of the Department of Defense—the DIA and the National Security Agency (NSA)—and are designated as combat support agencies. When they deploy, they fall under the supported command's director of intelligence (in this case CENTCOM's). The CIA, on the other hand, is an independent agency that works only with the CINC, not with the director of intelligence. In fact, the CIA calls its officer the representative of the Director of Central Intelligence (DCI), not the representative of the CIA itself. There is a difference. The DCI is also the director of the CIA. As such, this official not only heads the CIA but exercises operational oversight of an intelligence community made up of numerous organizations with some intelligence function, 75 percent of which are resident in the Department of Defense. The line between the two functions (DCI and CIA director) exists but is blurred, often purposely by CIA officers who wish to conduct their activities under the mantel of the entire intelligence community or in the name of the president.

For the most part, all three agencies support the command in their own particular specialties in a harmonious relationship. Occasionally, though, there are problems. For example, the DCI representative received the *National Intelligence Daily*. The *NID* is a product of the entire intelligence community (primarily the CIA, the DIA, and the NSA, who must all coordinate on the items in the report). When the *NID* arrived in Riyadh, the DCI representative usually took it directly to the CINC without allowing the director of intelligence to see it. In fact, the director of intelligence did not normally have access to the *NID* until after the morning intelligence briefing to the CINC. Thus the CINC had the benefit of the national intelligence community's analysis and collection not available in theater while the intelligence director, who had not yet seen the *NID*, was briefing him. Often Schwarzkopf would contradict the intelligence briefers with information from the *NID* that they had not yet seen but to which they were entitled. This unprofessional behavior was specifically cited in both the CENTCOM and Department of Defense reports on the conduct of the war. The CIA has vowed to correct this arrangement.

As the situation stabilized and the Iraqis became less of a perceived threat to Saudi Arabia with the increase of U.S. and coalition force levels, it became obvious that the defensive posture adopted by the coalition would have to give way to some final resolution of the crisis. Neither the senior civilian leadership nor the military leadership believed that the indefinite deployment of hundreds of thousands of American troops to Saudi Arabia was politically sustainable.

Gen. H. Norman Schwarzkopf and the author.

Iraq's military attaché to the United States, Brig. Gen. Nabil Khalil Sa'id, and the author, in 1988 at a reception in Washington, D.C.

The Al-Husayn missile—modified from the Soviet Scud—used against Iran in 1988 and against Israel and Saudi Arabia in 1991.

The restored Gate of Ishtar at entrance to ruins of ancient Babylon.

Iranian rockets captured at Al-Faw—note the labels saying "parts of bull-dozer" on the shipping box.

The Qadisiyah Martyrs' Memorial in Baghdad, with names of the hundreds of thousands of Iraqi soldiers killed in the eight-year war with Iran.

The Iraqi school used as Iranian divisional headquarters on the Al-Faw Peninsula, after its liberation in April 1988.

Iranian field hospital where chemical injuries were treated during the liberation of the Al-Faw Peninsula by Iraqi troops in April 1988.

Iranian gun, built in North Korea, used by Iranian forces to shell Kuwaiti oil fields from the occupied Al-Faw Peninsula in 1987 and 1988.

Iraqi military vehicles and stolen Kuwaiti property caught by U.S. pilots on the "Highway of Death."

Kuwait, 1991—oil wells set on fire by retreating Iraqi troops.

The author and Saudi counterparts at Safwan Airfield following its capture by the U.S. Army's 1st Infantry Division, the "Big Red One."

The author introduces Iraqi Lt. Gen. Sultan Hashim Ahmad Al-Jabburi to Gen. Norman Schwarzkopf (not visible behind Humvee), Safwan, Iraq, 3 March 1991.

5

Washington

Throughout Operation Desert Shield—the defense of Saudi Arabia—all members of the American forces, particularly those on the CENT-COM headquarters staff at the Saudi MODA building, were cautioned repeatedly by senior officers against discussing or even mentioning any offensive planning to liberate Kuwait. The official position stated that U.S. forces were in Saudi Arabia to assist the kingdom's armed forces in its defense. The liberation of Kuwait by military means was not part of the mission at that time. Among ourselves, we referred to the coming offensive as the "O word."

However, in a small isolated room in the bunker under the MODA building, a group of officers known as the "Jedi Knights" were beginning to develop the offensive plan to liberate Kuwait that would eventually become Desert Storm. The Jedis were hand-picked graduates of the U.S. Army School of Advanced Military Studies, an intensive postgraduate military operations program reserved for the army's brightest officers. A senior British plans officer was assigned to this group.

About half a mile away in a basement room of the Royal Saudi Air Force headquarters building, a similar group of U.S. Air Force planners had been developing since mid-August a massive air campaign to achieve a spectrum of effects, depending on the specific objectives decided in Washington. This room, to which access was severely restricted, was known as the "Black Hole." Although the planning was supposedly conducted with the knowledge of only a few senior members of the staff, almost everyone in the headquarters had some idea of what was going on.

In early October, the president asked the secretary of defense for options to liberate Kuwait. At this time, all planning in Riyadh was based on, and strictly limited to, the force level present in or moving to the theater. Thus planning figures included only the U.S. XVIII Airborne Corps consisting of the 82d Airborne Division, the 101st Airborne Division (Air Assault), and the 24th Infantry Division (Mechanized); the 1st Marine Division; the UK 7th Armoured Division; an Arab armored corps consisting of the Egyptian 3d Armored and 4th Mechanized Infantry Divisions and the Syrian 9th Armored Division; and units of the Royal Saudi Land Force and the SANG.

With only these forces available, the Jedis determined that the sole feasible attack option was directly into Iraqi strength in Kuwait. While the planners preferred a flanking maneuver to the west of Iraqi force concentrations, the movement was not logistically sustainable with the forces on hand, nor was there enough combat power to split the forces into the different attack elements required for such a maneuver. In any case, the task was to develop a plan with available forces.

The planning, both air and ground, was complicated by yet another requirement. General Schwarzkopf issued instructions to the planning cells that the final plan could not have any critical objectives dependent on non-American troops, with the exception of the British units. He later expanded this exemption to include French forces when they came under American command. In other words, when the attack was launched, American lives were not to be dependent on the success or failure of foreign troops to meet their objectives. Therefore, all key objectives had to be taken by American forces.

General Schwarzkopf's departure from the theater to brief the plan to the president would have been too noticeable to the coalition and might cause unnecessary rumors. In his place, he decided to send his chief of staff, marine major general Robert Johnston, to Washington to brief the leadership on the offensive planning. Schwarzkopf himself handpicked the members of the briefing team to accompany Johnston. He chose the air campaign planner, air force brigadier general Buster Glosson, ground campaign planner (and head of the "Jedi Knights") army colonel Joe Purvis, and me as the intelligence officer to set the stage by describing the current military situation and Iraqi capabilities.

We gave Schwarzkopf a dry run of the briefing we planned to give to the secretary of defense, the chairman of the Joint Chiefs of Staff, and the four service chiefs. After making some minor changes in the briefing, Schwarzkopf delivered his final instructions. He concluded with strict orders that the briefers were not to present their own opinions—we were to go to Washington to present General Schwarzkopf's briefing. In fact, he said, if any of us ventured our own opinions, he personally would call the secretary of whatever military branch we happened to be in and have us thrown out of the service. The general stressed that this was an important briefing, that decisions impacting the lives of American troops would be based on this event. He also told us we would probably end up briefing the president. Then he cracked a big smile and remarked, "Now that I have threatened your careers, do you have any questions?"

We flew to Washington on the CINC's EC-135 command aircraft, which featured dinner with wine, a welcome change. The four briefing officers (Johnston, Glosson, Purvis, and I) sat in the aircraft's well-appointed conference area. During the flight, we went over the briefings again to make sure that all four presentations agreed with each other and properly reflected General Schwarzkopf's views. Both Johnston and Glosson were familiar with our previous cooperative relationship with the Iraqis and were aware that I had spent considerable time on the ground in Baghdad and the battlefields of southern Iraq during the Iran-Iraq War. I was peppered with questions about the city, Iraqi military capabilities and operations, life in Iraq, and my opinions about the intentions of the Iraqis in a variety of hypothetical situations. Glosson was particularly interested in the Iraqi government buildings that I had visited and the bridges across the Tigris flowing through the center of town. Almost all of these buildings and bridges were later destroyed by F-117 air strikes.

At one point in the free-flowing discussion of planned air attacks on Iraq, General Johnston asked Glosson about the dangers and risks associated with bombing chemical, biological, and nuclear research and production facilities. Johnston was concerned especially about the release of chemical and biological warfare agents into the atmosphere and the risks to the surrounding population. Glosson explained that air force planners in Washington had done extensive research and computer modeling with the Department of Energy on just that question.

While there is always some risk associated with breaching the integrity of these types of facilities, accurate strikes with incendiary devices cause most of the agent to be burned off. It was assessed that risk to the surrounding civilian population was minimal since most of these facilities were built in relatively isolated areas for security reasons. Despite that assessment, there was extensive debate in air force circles about the acceptability of any risk of this sort. In the end, the risk was deemed acceptable because of the high priority attached to the destruction of the Iraqi weapons of mass destruction programs. Although the stated purpose of the offensive operation was the liberation of Kuwait, the United States wanted to reduce the ability of Iraq to threaten its neighbors (both Arab and Israeli) with either conventional or advanced weapons. All known chemical, biological, and nuclear research and production facilities were added to the target list.

We arrived in Washington late in the afternoon. The next day we briefed in the "Tank," the Pentagon briefing room reserved for the secretary of defense, the chairman of the Joint Chiefs of Staff, and the service chiefs. All of them were present, plus some of the secretary's key civilian advisors and the Joint Chiefs directors of intelligence and operations. We presented the briefing as we had rehearsed it in Riyadh.

I led off with the intelligence overview of what the current Iraqi situation was and what the CENTCOM analysts predicted it would be in thirty days, based on continued Iraqi troop deployments and public statements. According to CENTCOM analysis, we were looking at an Iraqi force structure in the Kuwait Theater of Operations (KTO) of as many as fifty divisions. I was careful to explain that fifty Iraqi divisions sounded more ominous than it was. All but twelve of these divisions were pure infantry with little armored support and were not at 100 percent strength, usually more like 65 percent. Although this still presented a formidable Iraqi force, the highly mobile and firepower-rich U.S. units supported by self-propelled artillery and coordinated army and air force air power would outflank or maneuver through these basically immobile Iraqi infantry divisions. This doctrine was called the "air-land battle" and was developed and exercised extensively in the 1970s and 1980s to fight the Soviets in Europe; it represented the latest concepts in American military thought to take advantage of all facets of existing technology. The main concern of American planners was the Iraqi heavy (armored or mechanized infantry) divisions, in both regular army corps and the Republican Guard Forces Command. We had detailed information on the elaborate Iraqi obstacle and minefield belts, which we gained through photoreconnaissance and debriefings of Iraqi deserters. Since I had coordinated my presentation with DIA analysts, my briefing generated no questions or contentious issues.

General Glosson then described the strategic air campaign, a four-phased coordinated attack plan designed to cripple Iraqi command and control, eliminate the integrated air defenses throughout Iraq and Kuwait, then later concentrate on Iraqi frontline forces prior to and during the coalition ground offensive. After Glosson finished, Colonel Purvis briefed the direct ground assault into Kuwait by U.S. Army and Marine forces. Purvis explained that while this was not the ideal method to attack the Iraqis, given the forces available to CENTCOM at the time, it was the only feasible option. There were numerous questions about the plan to attack into the main Iraqi force in Kuwait. Purvis explained that the planning cell had considered an attack up the western flank of the Iraqi lines, up the Wadi Al-Batin depression that forms the border between Kuwait and Iraq. This option was not logistically supportable with the resources either currently present or en route. Given the available resources, a direct attack into the center of the Iraqi lines was the only feasible choice.

Gen. Al Gray, commandant of the Marine Corps, expressed his dissatisfaction that the marines would not be making an amphibious landing on the beaches south of Kuwait City. The idea had been rejected earlier by Schwarzkopf. Since an amphibious landing is one of the most difficult military maneuvers to execute successfully, it is usually very costly in terms of casualties. It was assumed that this would be the case in an amphibious landing on the heavily mined beaches of Kuwait.

While the idea of an amphibious landing in Kuwait had been rejected, we did not want the Iraqis to know that. A major deception program to convince the Iraqis that we were planning such an attack on the Kuwaiti coast had been underway since September 1990. The deception plan was developed to force the Iraqis to maintain large numbers of forces along the coast to repel the marines until the beginning of the air campaign. Once the air campaign started, Iraqi forces would be unable to move the units west from the coast to the area of the main attack. In late 1990, when we detected that Iraqi forces were strengthening coastal defenses in anticipation of a marine landing, it was decided to continue a series of amphibious landing exercises to complement the ongoing deception plan.

General Johnston concluded the briefing by presenting General Schwarzkopf's assessment of the situation. Given available forces and resources, CENTCOM was prepared to execute the plan on order; however, estimated American casualties could be as high as twenty thousand. The unspoken point of this portion of the briefing was that additional forces would likely be needed to accomplish the liberation of Kuwait with the number of casualties acceptable to the American leadership and, more importantly, to the American people. Secretary Cheney ended the discussions with the words, "Thank you, gentlemen. Let's go see the president."

The next day we drove to the White House, where Secretary Cheney and General Powell met us. General Powell took the opportunity to speak with General Glosson about the air campaign. He stressed to Glosson that it was important Glosson not make the air campaign sound so easy and attractive that the leadership might opt to execute it in isolation or execute it prematurely.

We waited in the briefing room while Secretary of State James Baker, National Security Advisor Brent Scowcroft, his deputy Bob Gates, White House Chief of Staff John Sununu, and Vice President Dan Quayle gathered and traded good-natured jibes. After a few minutes, President Bush strode in purposely and asked Cheney, "What have you got for me?" Cheney explained that General Powell had brought a briefing team from CENTCOM headquarters in Riyadh representing General Schwarzkopf. Bush nodded at Powell and walked over to the team standing in the rear of the crowded room. Powell introduced us to the president and told him that I would begin the briefing with the intelligence picture.

My portion of the briefing was to set the stage for the presentation of the air campaign and ground-battle plans. It was the least controversial presentation and thus should draw the fewest questions. Easy, I thought. After all, I had successfully briefed a much tougher audience in the tank the day before—the country's five senior general officers (including the chief of my parent service) made for a much more nerve-wracking experience.

No sooner had I started than an aide came in and whispered something to the president, after which he excused himself for a few minutes.

When he returned, he appeared to be a bit distracted and apologized, explaining that he had been on the telephone to French president Mitterand. As he turned his attention back to the briefing, I described in detail the construction of the Iraqi defensive lines. When I moved on to the next topic, which was Iraqi command and control of forces in the region, Bush stopped me and asked me to repeat the description of the Iraqi defenses. In the ensuing questions and answers with the president (his questions, my answers), I mentioned that I had been in Iraqi trenches and defensive positions around Al-Basrah during the Iran-Iraq War. Bush looked inquiringly at Cheney and Powell. Cheney shook his head as if to say, "Don't pursue this, Mr. President." It appeared that the military cooperation with Iraq that had seemed such a good idea in 1987 and 1988 might come back to haunt us politically.

At the completion of my portion of the briefing, I asked the president if there were any additional questions. He asked about morale of the Iraqi troops in Kuwait. I said that all our indications were that morale was low, but this was based on interrogations of the very few deserters available at that time. He asked if, based on my experience with the Iraqis, it was my opinion that they would fight. Remembering the admonishment from General Schwarzkopf about voicing personal opinions, and the fact that our plans were based on the CENTCOM assumption that the Iraqis would fight if attacked, I hesitated. General Powell, aware of Schwarzkopf's proscription on giving our opinions, sensed my predicament. In a gesture that I will always appreciate, Powell leaned forward into my line of sight and nodded. I told the president that based on what I had seen in the defense of Al-Basrah in 1987, the Iraqis would probably not fight hard to defend Kuwait from a coalition attack. However, once we had pressed the attack into Iraq, we should plan for stiff resistance, especially if we approached the major population center of Al-Basrah. Bush nodded and thanked me, and I sat down.

General Glosson followed with the air campaign—a campaign that later proved to be very effective. Before we had left Riyadh, Schwarzkopf had warned General Glosson (as had Powell not an hour earlier) that the air campaign sounded too inviting and told him to make sure the briefing was an accurate portrayal of our capabilities. Concerns were already mounting that if air power sounded so effortless, it might be employed prematurely. These concerns had been echoed in the tank as well. Glosson deftly explained the various air options available to the president, one combat pilot to another.

Colonel Purvis then briefed the planned ground attack into the heart of Iraqi troop strength in Kuwait. After he completed his presentation, the main point of controversy came up. Scowcroft, a retired air force lieutenant general, asked why didn't we "just move out to the west" in a flanking maneuver rather than assault directly into the main Iraqi force. As he voiced this observation, he made a sweeping gesture with his left arm. Purvis, who had anticipated this question, explained that to "just move out to the west" was in fact the preferred option but that it entailed a massive flanking maneuver and required much more logistic capability than was projected to be available. Cheney and Powell remained silent. I suspect this was part of the overall plan to convince the president to commit additional forces to the effort.

President Bush took in all the discussions of the flanking maneuver and then struck at the heart of the matter by asking Cheney and Powell if American force levels were sufficient for the liberation of Kuwait. Powell explained that Schwarzkopf had been instructed to develop a plan based on the number of troops and units projected to be in theater. Given those figures, the direct attack was the best option but might cost up to twenty thousand casualties. Bush looked at Cheney and said, "What you are telling me is that Schwarzkopf needs more forces, right?" Powell answered for the secretary and said that Schwarzkopf was prepared to execute the plan as briefed but that additional forces would ensure the liberation of Kuwait with many fewer American casualties. Bush nodded. Powell continued that an additional corps, or as many as four divisions, would do the job. Bush again nodded, thanked everyone, stated that he had some decisions to make, and departed.

On the flight back to Riyadh, we were joined by Lt. Col. (now Brigadier General) Dave Deptula, Glosson's lead air-campaign planner and the officer most familiar with the detailed specifics of the campaign. During the return flight to Riyadh, we reviewed the briefing we had given the president. General Glosson was confident that the air power portion had gone well, but we were not sure we had convinced President Bush to provide more ground forces. The answer to that question came less than one month later.

In November 1990, just two days after the U.S. elections, Bush ordered the deployment of the U.S. Army's pride and joy, the VII Corps, from garrisons in Germany to Saudi Arabia. The VII Corps was equipped with the "latest and greatest" weaponry in the army inventory; after all, this corps had stood toe-to-toe with the Soviets through the entire Cold War. The corps was to be augmented by the 1st Infantry Division from its garrisons in Germany and Fort Riley, Kansas, and by the 1st Cavalry Division from Fort Hood, Texas, bringing over four and a half state-of-the-art heavy divisions to the fray. The largest U.S. armored force since World War II was headed for the Gulf.

In December, the entire 2d Marine Division marched in formation from Camp Lejuene, North Carolina, to embarkation points in a highly publicized ceremony carried live on CNN. The message would not go unnoticed in Baghdad—the Iraqis knew of, and feared, the U.S. Marines. With two thirds of the entire Marine Corps being sent to the Gulf, and the army's VII Corps joining the XVIII Airborne Corps already there, the United States was committing over three corps to what would eventually be a coalition of almost five corps. Additional U.S. Air Force fighter and bomber wings were ordered to the region, and for the first time in the history of naval aviation, the U.S. Navy prepared to position six large-deck aircraft carriers in the Persian Gulf and the Red Sea, representing almost half of the navy's air assets. CENTCOM was already planning the now-famous "left hook."

6

Amman

For years prior to the Iraqi invasion of Kuwait, the U.S. military relationship with Jordan had been very close—much closer than with any other Arab country. Jordanian officers attended numerous military schools in the United States. American officers attended Jordanian military schools and served exchange tours with Jordanian military units. Joint training exercises in the Jordanian desert were a common event.

I consider myself fortunate to have served as an advisor to a Jordanian reconnaissance battalion in 1984, although I am not sure who was advising whom. I say that because, man for man, the Jordanian armed forces stand among the best of the armed forces of the Middle East. They are professional, albeit few in number. They have the distinction of being the only Arab army to have taken ground in battle from the Israelis and held it. The Royal Jordanian Air Force, now far outclassed by the state-of-the-art American-built fighters of the Israeli Air Force, has at least one ace pilot with more than five confirmed kills. The history of the Jordanian military goes back to the creation of Transjordan (now the Hashemite Kingdom of Jordan) after World War I and the legendary Arab Legion created by British soldier Sir John Bagot Glubb. In fact, British officers served in the Legion until the 1960s.

Every year, meetings are held between senior U.S. Department of Defense officials and military officers and their counterparts in countries to which the United States provides any type of military assistance, training, or funds. The major recipient of American military largesse is Israel, closely followed by Egypt, with Greece and Turkey a far-distant third and fourth. This pattern of aid underscores the importance the United States attaches to the nations of the eastern Mediterranean—the volatility of the region and the political power of these nations' American constituents or lobbies. Far down the list of aid recipients is the Hashemite Kingdom of Jordan, ruled until his death in 1999 by one of world's longest-reigning monarchs, His Majesty King Hussein. Hussein was one of only two rulers in the Middle East who can make a credible claim of being a direct descendent of the Prophet Muhammad. The other is King Hasan of Morocco, not Saddam Husayn, as claimed by the blatantly false propaganda spewing forth from Baghdad.

In 1990, the U.S.-Jordan joint military commission meeting scheduled for the fall in Amman was canceled. The reason was King Hussein's strong and vocal support of Saddam Husayn—not for Saddam's invasion of Kuwait but for the Iraqi leader personally. It was decided in Washington that a military-to-military meeting with the Jordanians, now supporters of Iraq, would be inappropriate while hundreds of thousands of American troops were deploying to the deserts of Saudi Arabia to be arrayed against the Iraqis. American military aid to Jordan was suspended. It would take years for the United States to forgive the perceived treachery of the Jordanians.

The history of the creation of the nations of Jordan and Iraq after World War I is interwoven. Both began as kingdoms established by the British under their mandate as a reward to two Hashemite brothers, Faysal and 'Abdallah (King Hussein's grandfather), who had helped Col. Thomas Lawrence (more popularly known as "Lawrence of Arabia") wage a rear-area campaign against the Ottoman Turks.[1] Jordan and Iraq even tried a federation in the late 1950s. Eventually, a series of revolutions in Iraq overthrew the monarchy and introduced a long string of dictators, the latest being Saddam Husayn. In Jordan, despite early Palestinian attempts fostered by the followers of the Mufti of Jerusalem to overthrow the Hashemite monarchy—King 'Abdallah was assassinated by a Palestinian Arab in 1951—Jordan remains the Hashemite Kingdom.

Despite the difference in systems of government, there was, and is, a bond between the Iraqis and Jordanians. On the military side, mutual admiration has always existed. The Iraqis, regarded as tough and disciplined, saw the Jordanians as a small but technically proficient, professional military force. Although we had no concrete evidence of it, we in the Defense Department had always assumed that there was cooperation between the two nations' militaries. This fact was confirmed for me when I was serving as an advisor and my Jordanian battalion commander said, "Captain Rick, you must realize that everything you tell us, our brothers the Iraqis will know." Four years later, in 1988, we used that cooperation to our advantage.

In the spring of 1988, the Iranians were preparing for their annual spring offensive, this year aimed at seizing Al-Basrah. It was the consensus of Middle East analysts that Iraqi forces were facing a potential devastating defeat if the Iranians assaulted the city.[2] Prohibited by policy from warning the Iraqis of the impending serious threat to Al-Basrah, I recalled the words of my Jordanian commander, "You must realize . . . the Iraqis will know." A trip to brief King Hussein was arranged. In the late 1980s, briefings for the king were routine and occurred several times a year. In April 1988, I traveled to Amman and was afforded an audience with His Majesty at the Hashimiyah, the palace complex overlooking the city. The briefing covered a variety of topics, including the situation in Iraq. I assume the information was relayed to Baghdad.

However, by 1990, just two and a half years later, the situation between Jordan and the United States had changed dramatically. Iraq had invaded Kuwait, and King Hussein appeared to be siding with Saddam. Many political analysts concluded that the king had little choice. About 60 percent of the population of Jordan is composed of Palestinians, many poor. Many of Jordan's Palestinians had gone to Kuwait to take menial jobs and were not kindly treated by their wealthy Kuwaiti employers. They were not permitted to take their families or establish permanent residency.

Additionally, Jordan stood to lose a great amount of revenue from Iraqi use of the Jordanian port of 'Aqabah. Since the beginning of the Iran-Iraq War in 1980 and the closing of the Shatt Al-'Arab, 'Aqabah had been Iraq's primary port, needed for bringing in arms and food. Saddam Husayn had successfully tied his takeover of Kuwait to the Palestinian problem—at one point he offered to leave Kuwait when Israel left "Palestine." Although in the West this sounded ludicrous, in the Israeli-occupied territories of the West Bank and in Palestinian ghettos of Jordan's cities it was well received. Saddam became a folk hero.

Since there was to be no joint military commission meeting that fall of 1990, the U.S. ambassador to Jordan, Roger Harrison, asked that General Schwarzkopf provide him an update on the situation in the Gulf. Now on loan to Schwarzkopf's staff in Riyadh, I met the two major criteria to fly to Amman and brief the ambassador—I had packed a suit when I deployed to the theater, and I still had a valid Jordanian visa in my passport from earlier travels. I arrived in Amman early on 22 October. There to meet me at the airport was a friend and colleague, army attaché Lt. Col. Rich Mulhern, who invited me to join him and his wife for dinner that evening. I am glad I went, for it was the last time that I would ever see Rich. He was killed in northern Iraq while aboard one of two helicopters mistakenly downed by American fighter pilots in 1994.

The next day, I briefed Ambassador Harrison and his country team on the current situation in the Kuwait Theater of Operations. Overall, the briefing was well received. I could not discuss the offensive options that were being developed in Riyadh and certainly not the fact that General Schwarzkopf was about to get the premier heavy armored corps in the U.S. military, the VII Corps, which had been garrisoned in Germany since the end of World War II.

The ambassador was upset with several items that impacted on "his" country. I had stated in the briefing that CENTCOM was concerned that the Jordanians might be sharing intelligence with the Iraqis on U.S. and coalition forces deployed to Saudi Arabia and the Gulf. We had reports from the Saudi GID that the Jordanian military attaché in Riyadh was actively collecting information on U.S. and coalition troop deployments to Saudi Arabia, focusing on the location of command and control facilities.[3] Although the Saudis thought that the information was being gathered to support a possible Jordanian entry into the war on the Iraqi side, CENTCOM assessed that the information was being collected on behalf of the Iraqi DMI. The Iraqi military attaché in Riyadh had been expelled after the Iraqi invasion of Kuwait.[4]

The second item that displeased the ambassador was speculation that Jordanian officers might be training Iraqi air defense crews to operate the American-made "Improved HAWK" (I-HAWK) surface-to-air missile systems the Iraqis had captured intact from the Kuwaitis during the invasion in August. The I-HAWK was the principal weapon in the Jordanian air defense system, and the Jordanians were proficient in its use. Although there was no proof that they were conducting such training,

CENTCOM had decided to take the potential threat seriously. The I-HAWK, despite being somewhat dated, was regarded by U.S. pilots as one of the world's most dangerous air defense weapons. Virtually all I-HAWKs fired in combat had hit their targets. I-HAWKs in the hands of Jordanian-trained Iraqi crews could pose a serious threat to American and coalition flyers.

The ambassador was furious that we were briefing possible Jordanian complicity with the Iraqis, and he demanded that we remove these items from the briefing, claiming that this type of inflammatory information would seriously damage future relations with Jordan. General Schwarzkopf, however, was more concerned with potential threats to American airmen than with placating diplomats. The item remained in the CENTCOM briefing, and the ambassador remained unhappy.

After the war, during coalition inspection of vacated Iraqi positions, boxes of munitions with Jordanian markings and contract numbers were found. The soldiers who found the Jordanian munitions boxes claimed that dates were stenciled on the boxes indicating that the materiel had been transshipped to Iraq during Desert Shield; however, the soldiers did not seize any of the boxes or photograph the areas bearing these incriminating dates. During the Iran-Iraq War, the Jordanians were a conduit for large quantities of weapons shipped through the port of 'Aqabah. We could not be sure if these boxes were left over from the Iran-Iraq War, or if they had been shipped to Iraq during Desert Shield.

However, it was inevitable that sooner or later, given the dynamics of the Middle East peace process, the United States would have to repair its damaged relations with Jordan. The matter of possible Jordanian complicity with Iraq seemed to fade away after the war. In 1996, I spoke with Jordanian officers who admitted being in Baghdad in late 1990. Although they never specifically discussed the I-HAWK issue with me, they stated that they and other senior Jordanian officers familiar with American air power capabilities and doctrine had repeatedly warned the Iraqis of the certain devastation that the United States could inflict on them. They had explained to their Iraqi colleagues that in the entire war with Iran, Iraq had never faced a serious air threat, that the war was primarily an infantry contest. According to the Jordanian officers, the Iraqis could not comprehend the capabilities of American air power. Saddam's military intelligence chief Wafiq Al-Samarra'i, after his defection to the West, described Saddam's amazement that air strikes could be so accurate and devastating. The Iraqi DMI assessment prepared after the war stated that the air campaign had rendered the Iraqi army defenseless and was the main factor in Iraq's defeat.

Following the briefings at the embassy, I spent a day in Amman while waiting for my flight back to Riyadh. I had spent a lot of time in Jordan over the years, much of it in Amman or its environs. It was different now. Signs of support for Saddam Husayn were everywhere—on buses, taxis, cars, and even graffiti on walls. Young men wore T-shirts proclaiming in Arabic "I am a Palestinian—I was born on 2 August" (the date of the Iraqi invasion of Kuwait). The images of King Hussein, Saddam Husayn, and Yasir 'Arafat superimposed in the sky over one of the most notable symbols of Islam, the Dome of the Rock, was a common item. Small wooden models of the Al-Husayn missile were for sale at all local souks. For the first time ever, I was uncomfortable to be an American on the streets of Amman.

During my stay in Amman, Saddam released several of the Americans he was using as human shields, at the behest of an Iraqi-American friendship organization headed by a doctor from Arlington, Virginia. I was staying at the Intercontinental Hotel, located directly across the street from the U.S. embassy in Amman. I knew the doctor from Iraqi embassy functions in Washington, and he recognized me in the lobby. He told me that in his meeting with Saddam Husayn in Baghdad just a few days earlier, the Iraqi leader said he had no intention of relinquishing control of Kuwait.

The doctor also gave me some sad news. A friend of us both, Brig. Gen. Nabil Khalil Sa'id, the former Iraqi military attaché at the Iraqi embassy in Washington, had been executed as a probable agent of the Americans. These charges were no doubt based on his years in Washington and his role in the cooperation between our military services in 1988. He and I had worked together closely, and I considered Nabil a fine officer who had represented his country well under difficult circumstances. Again, an enemy, a friend.

When I returned to Riyadh, I wrote a short report for General Schwarzkopf recounting my observations of the situation in Jordan. Based on his handwritten comments on my report, I surmised that he too was surprised at the turn of events in a country that had been previously a key ally and a bastion of pro-American sentiment in the Arab world.

Not until 1994 did King Hussein reverse his position on Iraq and denounce the regime of Saddam Husayn. Although he had been distancing himself from the Saddam regime after the Iraqi defeat in 1991, the event that crystallized the king's about-face was the defection of Husayn Kamil in August 1995. During his meetings with King Hussein, Husayn Kamil provided a chilling picture of Saddam Husayn's excesses and the Iraqi leader's displeasure that the Jordanian monarch appeared to be mending fences with the U.S. political and military establishments. Since then, and until he died of cancer in 1999, King Hussein remained firmly in the anti-Saddam camp.

7

The Sheikh and
the Courier

In late October 1990, following our briefing of the president regarding
General Schwarzkopf's proposed plans, the Jedi Knights continued
planning the ground offensive. As the discussions intensified between
General Schwarzkopf and Washington on the number of additional
forces that would be required to liberate Kuwait, it became obvious that
sooner rather than later, we would be on the attack. One of the key issues
required for planning the ground offensive for the liberation of Kuwait
was the logistics support for the attacking army, marine, and coalition
ground forces—water, food, fuel, ammunition, thousands of other
items—and lots of it.

Everything that would be needed for ground operations in the
desert would have to be trucked to the area over a single highway called
the Tapline (Trans-Arabian Pipeline) Road, a two-lane road paralleling
the now-defunct oil pipeline from the Persian Gulf to ports on the
Mediterranean Sea. After the use of roadways as far west as possible, the
supplies would have to be trucked across the desert itself to the units
on the attack. As an example of the magnitude of the problem: at the
height of ground operations, the logistics system had to move ten million gallons of fuel every day, not to mention tons of food and hundreds of thousands of gallons of drinking water.[1]

After the decision by the president and secretary of defense to
deploy the VII Corps from garrisons in Germany to Saudi Arabia, the
Jedi Knights reverted to the preferred option of attacking Iraqi forces

in the Kuwait Theater of Operations (KTO) from the western flank rather than directly into the center of Iraqi strength in southwestern Kuwait. Despite press reports to the contrary, the "left hook," or the "Hail Mary," originated in that small room in MODA headquarters at CENTCOM, not in Washington.

The western flank option required accurate information on the trafficability of the terrain in southern Iraq. It was assessed that U.S. and British tanks and armored personnel carriers, being tracked vehicles, could traverse the terrain, but the question remained about the wheeled French tanks and coalition support vehicles. Of key concern: could the desert sands support the weight of the heavy five-thousand-gallon fuel tankers that would be needed to support two reinforced corps on the move?

The "school solution" was to send a special forces team clandestinely into the target area and take core soil samples for compression analysis. The problem was that thus far we had been successful in keeping secret the location of the main thrust of the attack. We had detected no indications that the Iraqis were aware of the intended axis of the main coalition attack to be executed by the VII Corps, although any student of American military doctrine could have guessed with a fair degree of accuracy—American doctrine is fairly straightforward. Still, Iraqi defectors told of planning to repel a coalition amphibious assault, led by the U.S. Marines, on the beaches of Kuwait and a thrust into the "shoulder" of Kuwait by U.S. Army and coalition armored forces.

Apparently, the ongoing deception campaign of an impending U.S. Marine amphibious landing on the Kuwaiti coast, reinforced by a series of exercises on beaches in Oman and Saudi Arabia, was having the desired effect. Therefore, it was determined that infiltrating special forces teams into the actual attack area might tip the Iraqis and cause a shift in their defensive planning, drawing forces away from the coast and concentrating on the area of the assault. Fewer Iraqi forces in the main attack area would mean fewer U.S. and coalition casualties. In January 1991, following heated discussions between General Schwarzkopf and his director of intelligence, special forces teams eventually did enter the areas prior to the ground offensive but well after the start of the air campaign.

Without actual soil samples, the challenge of determining the trafficability of denied terrain fell to the intelligence community, specifically to the CENTCOM director of intelligence, Brig. Gen. Jack Leide. He tasked the entire CENTCOM intelligence structure—headquarters, component intelligence staffs, national agency representatives, and theater collection organizations—to provide a reliable terrain analysis of the operational area. The area of interest extended from the Saudi Arabia-Kuwait-Iraq tri-border area centered in the northern Saudi town of Hafr Al-Batin out to the west for a distance of about a hundred and fifty miles. The primary area of concern was the VII Corps main attack axis, a ninety-mile zone to the west of the Hafr Al-Batin tri-border area. This all had to be done without alerting the Iraqis. The bulk of the task fell to the U.S. Army's 513th Military Intelligence Brigade, supported by a topographical engineering unit from Fort Bragg, North Carolina, that specialized in terrain analysis.

In addition to imagery and weather studies, a search was conducted of all available literature on the area. This included oil company reports from the 1930s and the fifty-year-old diaries of the famed English desert fighter, Sir John Bagot Glubb, or "Glubb-Pasha" as he was known throughout the region. His descriptions of maneuvering armored cars in the area and his descriptions of the density and passability of the sand-dune belts were very helpful.

Key resources in determining the trafficability of the terrain in the area were the people who traversed it on a daily basis—the bedouin. One of the enduring questions was where the loyalty of these nomadic Arabs would lie. As downed U.S. fliers were to find out later during Desert Storm, the direction of this allegiance was largely unpredictable. Some of the bedouin sided with Saddam Husayn, others with the coalition. Trying to determine loyalty based on tribal or clan lines was fruitless; virtually every tribe and clan had Iraqi, Saudi, and Kuwaiti branches, who are usually loyal to that government—but not always. Inside Iraq, the bedouin were promised large rewards for the capture of coalition special forces operating behind the lines or of downed coalition fliers. The money was an incentive, as was the knowledge that harboring coalition military personnel meant death for many in the tribe.

In November, just as General Schwarzkopf became more resolute in his demands for a reliable terrain analysis, a group of bedouin crossed the border from southern Iraq into Saudi Arabia through the "neutral zone." When the borders between the newly created Arab countries were arbitrarily drawn after the end of World War I, provisions were made for the nomadic bedouin to continue their way of life through the creation of neutral zones. The bedouin could cross borders through these zones without customs and immigration formalities. Months earlier, before the Iraqi invasion of Kuwait, this group's crossing of the border would have been a nonevent. Given the current situation, however, they were detained by Saudi forces and taken to the sprawling complex named King Khalid Military City, more commonly known as KKMC, near the desert oasis town of Hafr Al-Batin.

When he learned that the group had crossed the border from Iraq, General Schwarzkopf directed me to go to KKMC and thoroughly debrief the bedouin concerning the terrain. He further cautioned me to be careful not to give the impression that this was in any way a prelude to a coalition attack. General Schwarzkopf wanted the terrain information from people who had been there, and he placed his personal U.S. Air Force executive jet at my disposal to fly to KKMC to talk to the bedouin. On 18 November, CENTCOM intelligence analyst marine major Chris Ross and I flew to KKMC to meet with them.

I had worked extensively with officers from various Arab militaries and had found them to be generally proficient technically. But though I had spoken and socialized with bedouin before, I had never worked with them. This was to be a new experience. I quickly found that maps were a foreign concept to the bedouin. Try as I might, I could not get the bedu sheikh properly oriented to the map. Distances could only be estimated by how long it took to drive by Toyota truck (which has largely replaced the camel) between here and there. North, south, east, and west were meaningless. Every time I laid the map down on the ground and indicated north, the sheikh would turn the map ninety degrees counterclockwise and decree east to be north. I finally gave up and used terms such as "in the direction of Kuwait City," "in the direction of Mecca," or "in the direction of Hafr Al-Batin."

The bedouin may not have understood maps, but no one knew the actual desert terrain better; the sheikh and his sons were a wealth of current, reliable, and detailed information. They were able to delineate accurately the locations of sabkhas—muddy areas that are fed by underground water marshes and were impassable at this time of year—as well as surface salt flats that retain water and become slimy but are impassable only immediately following periods of rain. Our maps did not distinguish between the two areas, both appearing to be impassable desert swamps. With the bedouin's help, we were able to plot travers-able areas.

As for capacity of the desert terrain in the attack area to support the weight of the U.S. five-thousand-gallon Oshkosh heavy tanker, the sheikh's oldest son was the key contributor. I asked him about using vehicles in the area to the west of the Kuwait-Iraq border, and he replied that he did it all the time, year round, in his Chevrolet Caprice. The Caprice was the car of choice among many Saudis, Kuwaitis, and bedouin because it had a superior air-conditioning system that func-tioned well in the extreme desert heat. The plebeian Caprice remains popular to this day in Kuwait because in 1990, when many Kuwaitis drove into the desert and headed for Saudi Arabia to escape the invad-ing Iraqis, the automobile was able to travel where other, more expen-sive cars could not.

When I asked what he did for a living, the son replied with great dig-nity that he was an "international courier of small objects of great value, bringing people what they want." I somewhat jokingly remarked that in the United States, we might call such a person a smuggler. He smiled and said, "Please, sir, *smuggler* is such an ugly word." We agreed that he was a courier. But regardless of his trade, like most of the bedouin, he was an astute observer of terrain—able to estimate angles of slopes, the heights of dunes, the density of sand in different areas, weather pat-terns, the water retainability of different areas, and the sizes of stones in boulder-strewn areas. Armed with this information, the terrain spe-cialists and intelligence analysts were able to provide an educated assess-ment to General Schwarzkopf on where he could and could not send the heavy U.S. fuel tankers.

Had we gained the information required and not tipped our hand? I tried, but the word *bedouin* does not translate to "stupid." I asked the Saudi regional commander if the bedouin would be remaining in the Hafr Al-Batin area for the near future. He smiled and assured me that they would not be returning to Iraq until the "Kuwait situation" had been resolved.

The bedouin had provided useful information that, by some accounts, was critical to our understanding of the terrain. At our behest, the Saudis had detained the nomads from leaving KKMC and continu-ing their itinerant life in the desert. Although under Saudi laws they were due no compensation, we saw to it that the sheikh received something for his time and trouble. It is hard to find the right gift for bedouin, but the Saudis told us that the most prestigious item a sheikh could possess was a fifteen-hundred-gallon Mercedes water tanker. It was delivered soon after the end of the war, with the compliments of the United States Central Command.

Hail Mary and the Politics of Planning

After President Bush authorized the deployment of additional U.S. forces, virtually doubling the combat power available to General Schwarzkopf, ground offensive planning moved into a new phase. The Jedi Knights were now able to fully utilize their training and exploit the range of military capabilities and logistics provided by the addition of the VII Corps and the additional marine division. The preferred ground assault option—a flanking maneuver to the west of the Iraq-Kuwait border—would now be possible. The "Hail Mary" option was now a reality.

The president had announced his decision to the public, explaining that he was giving General Schwarzkopf the forces needed to execute an offensive action to liberate Kuwait. This was the first acknowledgment that the coalition—but in reality, the United States—was now committed to ejecting the Iraqis from Kuwait, by military action if necessary. Saddam immediately announced he was doubling the amount of Iraqi forces in the theater of operations to defend "Iraq's nineteenth province."

Following President Bush's announcement, the Saudis and other members of the coalition were brought into the offensive planning. This created new requirements, and headaches, for the planners. Not only did they have to satisfy senior U.S. leadership in Washington and the CENTCOM staff in Riyadh; now their work had to be coordinated with other members of the coalition, all with their own national agendas. For example, the United Kingdom insisted that its 7th Armoured Division be included in the main attack rather than being assigned to elements conducting supporting attacks or serving as tactical or corps reserves. The British insisted that because of political sensitivities in London, their troops had to be major participants in the main thrust. The Canadians, who contributed air and naval units to the coalition, prohibited their aircraft from entering either Kuwaiti or Iraqi air space. The Canadian fighters were permitted to fly defensive patrols over northern Saudi Arabia during offensive coalition air operations, thus freeing up other nations' fighters for operations over Iraq and Kuwait.

Other members of the coalition had requirements that had to be addressed as well. Syria, which had contributed its 9th Armored Division to be part of the "Arab Corps" with two Egyptian divisions, insisted that the division be used in reserve rather than in the actual assault against Iraqi troops. The exact reason for this demand was never clearly articulated, but the Syrians still used older-generation Soviet-made T-55 tanks. Thus they would probably face superior equipment in the Iraqi inventory and might not be able to keep up with the American-equipped Egyptian tank units. The Egyptians, who had for years used the T-55 tank, had gained access to American military equipment following Anwar Sadat's signing of the 1979 Camp David Accords treaty with Israel. By 1990, the Egyptians had acquired the very capable U.S. Army M-60A3 Patton tanks from American units that were receiving the state-of-the-art M-1 Abrams. After the war, Egyptian and Syrian troops took virtually every piece of usable Iraqi equipment they could find on the battlefields back home with them for use by their own forces.

Syrian participation in the coalition was interesting. It was through the efforts of U.S. Secretary of State James Baker and Egypt's President Husni Mubarak that Syria agreed to provide troops to the coalition. While no one expected the Syrian army's contribution to the coalition forces to markedly increase the combat power of the coalition, it nonetheless provided significant political impact, especially in the Arab world.

We were surprised to learn that the Syrians were sending their 9th Armored Division, commanded by Maj. Gen. 'Ali Habib, to Saudi Arabia. The 9th was garrisoned southwest of Damascus and was a primary unit tasked to defend the approach to Damascus from the Golan Heights. Although it was not one of Syria's premier units—such as the regime protection units around Damascus, whose mission was to defend against internal as well as external threats—it did weaken Syria's posture against Israel, which was regarded as its principal threat. One could make the argument that Syria's president, Hafiz Al-Asad, may have received assurances from the United States that Israeli forces would not take advantage of the situation. He may have reasoned that Syria's participation in a U.S.-led coalition, or at least its temporary alliance with Washington, would give any Israeli leader pause before attacking Syria.

With the exception of neighboring Lebanon, and an ill-fated incursion into Jordan in 1970, Syrian combat units had never been deployed outside Syria. Lebanon and Jordan could be reached by a series of good roads. However, the task of moving more than three hundred tanks and armored vehicles and the division's ten thousand men to Saudi Arabia was far beyond the logistic capabilities of the Syrian military. As part of the agreement to send troops, the division was to be moved by ship at Saudi expense, in much the same manner as the Egyptian units had been deployed to Saudi Arabia. Syrian military planners had to move the division from south of Damascus to the northern port of Latakia, a distance of almost two hundred fifty miles. The Syrian army had so few HETs—its primary means of moving armored formations—that relocation of the division from garrison to port would take weeks. At the suggestion of an American officer, the Syrians tried a method favored by U.S. (and Iraqi) logistics experts: movement of armor by rail. When the Israelis discovered that America had in this way vastly improved Syrian military logistics, they were furious and protested vehemently to the Defense Department.

Once in Saudi Arabia, the Syrians deployed the 9th Division with the Egyptians on the Kuwait-Saudi border, just east of the prewar Iraq-Kuwait border. With the positioning of the Syrian and Egyptian divisions close to the Iraqi lines, a serious concern was raised: the possible confusion on the battlefield between Soviet-made Iraqi equipment and identical Soviet-made Syrian and Egyptian equipment, similar to potential confusion between French Air Force and Iraqi Air Force Mirage F-1 fighter aircraft. Syrian and Egyptian forces, normally protected by Soviet-made air defense systems (missile and antiaircraft artillery) were ordered not to activate their air defense radars because the threat warning systems on U.S. and coalition aircraft would identify these signals as hostile. In the heat of battle, a pilot might mistakenly engage a Syrian or Egyptian air defense unit.

For the same reasons that the Syrians and Egyptians could not use their air defense systems, they could not bring helicopters or aircraft to provide close air support. To make up for this shortfall, U.S. Army officers were assigned as liaison with the Syrian and Egyptian commanders to coordinate any required U.S. air support. The methodology and capabilities of U.S. air support differed significantly from those of the Syrian or Egyptian armed forces. American "air-land battle" doctrine, refined and exercised for years, capitalized on the firepower of ground maneuver units and the flexibility of attack helicopters and fighter aircraft. Syrian commanders were exposed to the American doctrine, again much to the consternation of the Israelis. The Israelis believed that the Syrians would be able to apply lessons learned from the Americans to upgrade their air support capabilities for future conflicts with Israeli troops. The Syrian Air Force possesses very capable French-built Gazelle attack helicopters and Soviet-built Mi-25 "Hind" gunships.

Probably the most important planning decision was to exclude Arab or Muslim forces from participating in attacks into sovereign Iraqi territory. This decision—a U.S. political determination—was made to ease the inevitable and necessary future reconciliation in the region. The Arab and Muslim countries, which had to coexist in the area with the Iraqis, would be able to claim truthfully that they had not invaded a brother Arab state, unlike the Iraqis who had seized Kuwait.

According to the attack plans that were being drawn up, the U.S. XVIII Airborne Corps (augmented by the French 6th Armored Division) and the I Marine Expeditionary Force (composed of the 1st and 2d U.S. Marine Divisions) would attack simultaneously. The XVIII Corps and French forces would drive deep into Iraq on the western edge of the front, while the marines would push into Kuwait, attacking directly toward the airport and Kuwait City itself. These two attacks would focus and pin the Iraqis.

The next day, the U.S. VII Corps, augmented by the UK 7th Armoured Division and the U.S. 1st Infantry Division, would conduct the main assault into Iraq, driving north along the western side of the Iraq-Kuwait border. The VII Corps was to "close with and destroy" the Republican Guard units positioned astride the border to the north of the front lines. At the same time as the VII Corps attack, the Egyptian-Syrian corps

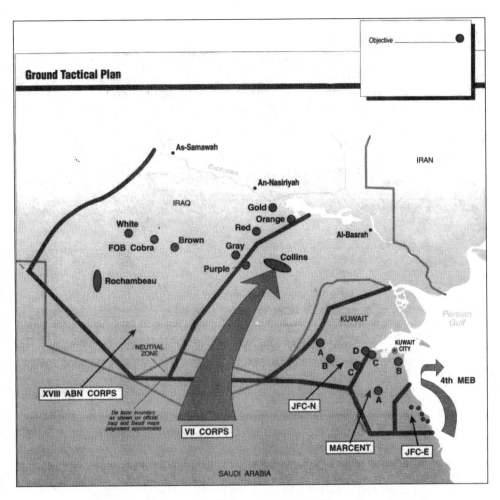

The ground offensive plan—the U.S. VII Corps would conduct the main assault to destroy the Republican Guard forces deployed northwest of Kuwait. *DOD*

(officially called Joint Forces Command–North) would launch a supporting assault immediately to the east of the VII Corps, moving into western Kuwait. Along the coast attacking into Kuwait was JFC-East, composed of the Saudis, the Kuwaitis, and their Arab and Muslim coalition partners. As planned, no Arab or Muslim forces ever attacked Iraq proper, although they did attack Iraqi forces in Kuwait. When it was all over, the only coalition countries with combat forces inside Iraq were the United States, the United Kingdom, and France.

Prior to the ground assault, Iraqi military intelligence had prepared an assessment of the coalition plan. Students of military history are fully aware of U.S. military doctrine—it is not elusive or complicated. American military planners have followed tenets developed by Civil War generals such as Thomas "Stonewall" Jackson. Not surprisingly, Iraqi military intelligence analysts prepared an assessment for Saddam Husayn that was very accurate. According to Saddam's military intelligence chief, Brig. Gen. Wafiq Al-Samarra'i, the assessment stated that American, British, and French forces would attack into Iraq north toward the Euphrates River, cutting the main supply route from Baghdad to Al-Basrah. The Iraqi forces in Kuwait and southern Iraq would be cut off and destroyed. The Iraqi intelligence chief had the unpleasant task of advising Saddam that given the projected effects of a devastating American-led air campaign, coalition ground forces would be successful in the postulated assault and Iraq would be defeated. The assessment also correctly stated that coalition forces would not attack as far as Baghdad.[1]

General Schwarzkopf reiterated one of his key planning instructions. As in the original plan written prior to the doubling of troop strength, he directed that the planners write a plan that did not place any critical action in the hands of anyone but American, British, or French forces. In other words, if all the other coalition allies failed to achieve their assigned objectives, the plan would still succeed on the strength of successful U.S.-British-French operations. It may sound elitist or insulting to our coalition allies, but Schwarzkopf wanted no American lives depending on the military capabilities of forces other than those in which he had absolute faith and confidence. The United States and the UK have probably the closest military relationship of any two countries in the world, both on a direct bilateral basis and as part of NATO. Further, the British armed forces are among the finest in the world.

France, while a political member of NATO, had not participated actively in NATO's military structure for some time, but it usually conducted parallel exercises with NATO during major NATO exercises. The French had established liaison offices at every significant NATO echelon and maintained its units in accordance with NATO standards. Schwarzkopf was familiar with the capabilities of both allies and knew they could be counted on to meet their mission objectives.

After the plan was written, it had to be coordinated with the coalition members since they had to live with it. CENTCOM coordinated with the British and the French, since they were now an integral part of the U.S. force structure. General Schwarzkopf provided a copy to General Khalid for coordination with the countries contributing units to the JFC. Khalid responded with two pages of comments on the plan. As was normal, I was called to the command section to provide a translation for Schwarzkopf. The memorandum was neatly typed and bore Khalid's signature. As I skimmed through the document, I was struck by Khalid's waffling, almost negative tone. His recommendations included the idea that we more fully exploit the airborne capabilities of U.S. forces and consider placement of Saudi units in different locations—both reasonable military suggestions from one general officer to another. However, what caught my eye—the real show stopper—was a recommendation that Schwarzkopf consider making the primary attack from Turkey into northern Iraq rather than from Saudi Arabia into Kuwait and southern Iraq. At about the time I saw this and snorted, General Schwarzkopf came into the office and got a Diet Pepsi, his favorite soft drink, from the refrigerator. He asked how the translation was coming. I said I had briefly scanned it and was puzzled by Khalid's suggestion that the main attack be from Turkey. Taken aback, Schwarzkopf responded, "What? Are you sure?"

I replied that I had only read a few sentences but that this was not a particularly tough translation and I should have it for him in a few minutes. He told me to bring it in to him the moment I was finished. Knowing this was an important piece of correspondence, I decided to take my time and produce a meticulous translation of the document. After about fifteen minutes, Schwarzkopf came out of his office and asked if I was done yet. I said I had translated it and was typing it up. He said to read it to him from my notes, which I did. As I had told him earlier, the document recommended that the main attack be mounted from Turkey. I could see both steam and disbelief rising as Schwarzkopf stormed back into his office. I finished typing the translation and gave it to the general. Becoming more furious as he read the text of the memorandum, he immediately headed for Khalid's office.

Schwarzkopf confronted Khalid and asked if he were serious about conducting the main attack from Turkey while Schwarzkopf was in the process of deploying in excess of five hundred thousand American troops to Saudi Arabia to launch an attack to liberate Kuwait. Khalid, seeing Schwarzkopf's anger over such a ludicrous proposal, attempted to shift the blame to me, claiming that Schwarzkopf's interpreter must have misunderstood the intent of that portion of the memorandum. The Arabic words that caused the confrontation between Schwarzkopf and Khalid are not ambiguous. The Arabic words *tanfiz al-hajum al-ra'isi min turkiyah* can only mean "execution of the main attack from Turkey."

Schwarzkopf said that his interpreter had explained the meaning of the Arabic text to him and his understanding was that the Saudis now wanted the main attack to come from the north, from Turkey, to create surprise among the Iraqi forces. The Saudi general claimed that he had meant the air campaign, not the ground assault. That was just as ridiculous as the ground assault. Khalid, appearing uncomfortable, said he would review the plan again and get back to Schwarzkopf. General Schwarzkopf describes this confrontation in his book *It Doesn't Take a Hero,* as does General Khalid in *Desert Warrior.* Schwarzkopf's recounting of the incident is the way I myself recall its happening.

A few days later, we received a memorandum from Khalid concurring with the plan as written. We were never sure how much coordination was done among the other nations contributing units to the Saudi-led Joint Forces Command.

Although Khalid had agreed with the plan, committing the kingdom to offensive action required the concurrence of the minister of defense and the king. The minister, Khalid's father and the king's brother, asked for a briefing on the plan so that he could approach the king for approval. The briefing would follow the same format we had used to brief President Bush in October. The intelligence briefing would lay out the situation, followed by briefings on the air campaign and then the ground-attack plan.

Schwarzkopf hosted the briefing. Since the minister's English was not as fluent as Khalid's, the briefing had to be translated into Arabic. Schwarzkopf thought it would be courteous if I gave the intelligence portion of the briefing in Arabic. I presented the briefing, as I did every day to the senior coalition command staff. The minister sat and listened; he then asked a few questions, which I answered. At the end of my presentation, he seemed to realize that we had been speaking Arabic. Turning to Schwarzkopf, he remarked that he was pleased and somewhat surprised that the United States had officers who could speak Arabic well enough to present a complex military briefing. Although the rest of the briefing was in English and had to be translated for the minister, Schwarzkopf had scored a political victory with a small gesture.

After concurrence from the JFC and the allies had been obtained, orders executing the plan were prepared. Ideas on paper now had to be turned into reality. The success of military operations is almost always based on the ability of logistics to support the operation. The American military possesses the finest logistics system in the world. Watching the tightly choreographed movements of hundreds of thousands of troops and hundreds of thousands of tons of supplies to staging areas is an education in management and in how to fight and win a war.

The question is often asked, "How could such a large number of troops and supplies be moved without detection by the Iraqis?" The answer is elusive. Iraqi intelligence services, like most in the Middle East, were concerned primarily with protection and survival of the current regime. The Iraqis did possess a credible foreign intelligence capability in the Directorate of Military Intelligence during the war with Iran. However, aggressive counterintelligence and internal security operations on the part of the Saudi Ministry of the Interior's *Mubahith* (literally, "Investigations," a three-department organization similar to the U.S. Federal Bureau of Investigation) deprived the DMI of most of its intelligence agents in the kingdom. Although the Saudis attempted to "double" some of the Iraqi agents they arrested—that is, to convince or compel them to work for Saudi intelligence against their former masters—this effort did not prove to be very successful. The Iraqi embassy in Riyadh had been closed shortly after the invasion of Kuwait in August and could not provide a platform for intelligence collection.

Further, prior to any movement of troops to staging areas for the ground assault into Kuwait and southern Iraq, the coalition air forces had cleared the skies of any Iraqi aircraft, including Iraqi reconnaissance aircraft. Although Soviet and Iraqi intelligence services had cooperated in the past, allowing Iraqis the benefit of Soviet satellite reconnaissance information, the Soviets apparently decreased their intelligence support during Desert Shield and Desert Storm. Soviet satellites were easily capable of detecting the coalition movement to the west in preparation for the "left hook." According to Saddam's military intelligence chief, information provided by the Russians on coalition troop movements was not accurate. Information was also provided to the Iraqi DMI by several cooperating services.

In addition to reports from the Jordanian military attaché in Saudi Arabia, the Iraqis received information from the Cuban and Yemeni military intelligence agencies.[2] But with no space reconnaissance capability of its own, having lost access to the commercial SPOT Image downlink, and only unreliable intelligence from its allies, Iraq was in effect blinded to coalition movements just south of its border.

9

Lessons in Air Power

Planning for the offensive continued into December and the Christmas–
New Year holiday season. The mood in Riyadh was somber, as most of
the American troops felt that war was becoming inevitable. The additional forces President Bush had ordered deployed to the Gulf were
starting to arrive—aircraft, ships, armored units, and marines.

The year-end holiday period is always a difficult time for American
servicemembers to be away from home and families. It was especially
difficult this time because as we prepared to go to war, it was not clear
what discussions and negotiations were taking place in the United
Nations or in other capitals of the world. We knew the Russians were trying to convince their long-time clients in Baghdad to make some sort of
diplomatic gesture to prevent a military confrontation. In Saudi Arabia,
we were waiting for the word on whether the situation was going to be
solved by diplomats or whether we would have to fight.

We did not have to wait long. Last-minute talks on 9 January in Geneva
between U.S. Secretary of State James Baker and his Iraqi counterpart,
Tariq 'Aziz, ended with no positive results.[1] The orders for war came from
the secretary of defense by courier shortly thereafter.

On the night of 16 January (in the Western Hemisphere; it was
already 17 January in the Gulf), Operation Desert Shield became Desert
Storm with massive air and missile attacks on targets throughout Iraq
and Kuwait. While the Iraqis were not surprised by the attacks, they
were overwhelmed by the severity and devastating effects. Although they

had fought the Iranians for eight years, and had been caught off guard by a small Israeli air raid in 1981, they had never been exposed to air power in the American context. The attacks were a complex orchestration of thousands of aircraft sorties—fighters, fighter-bombers, bombers, AWACS, electronic warfare, reconnaissance, aerial refueling tankers—from all U.S. services as well as several other countries, each playing a specified role at a particular time, place, altitude, speed, and a dozen other factors.

At the same time that a joint air force–army helicopter task force was destroying several Iraqi radar stations in the south to clear a path into Iraq for the swarms of combat planes gathering over northern Saudi Arabia, F-117 stealth fighters flying undetected over central Baghdad began precision air strikes on key command and control targets in the city. These targets included air defense centers, power generation stations, and communications facilities—those targets whose loss would "decapitate" the Iraqi war machine and allow coalition aircraft to take control of the skies over the entire country. Once air superiority, followed by air dominance, was achieved, coalition aircraft could strike targets across Iraq with relative impunity.

As soon as word reached Baghdad concerning the helicopter attack on the radar sites in the south, and just prior to the F-117 strikes, the skies lit up with a massive barrage of antiaircraft fire. The display broadcast live on CNN was sobering. As we watched the network's coverage of events in Baghdad from the command post, we feared that many aircraft and pilots would be lost. As it turned out, though the Iraqi gunners could not acquire the stealth fighters on their radar, they knew someone was dropping bombs or launching missiles, so they fired everything they had in blind attempts to hit something. The barrage was impressive—it became part of the CNN logo for their coverage of the war and the "brag shot" of their reporting—but ineffective. CNN's presence did serve at least one purpose that night, however. When the lead F-117 dropped a two-thousand-pound laser-guided bomb onto the main power generation plant in Baghdad, the network went off the air and the city went dark. We knew that particular strike had been a success.

The reaction among the Saudi officers in the Coalition Coordination, Communications, and Integration Center (C3IC)— most of whom had not been told prior to the H-hour that the air war was about to begin— was one of near incredulity. Although it was apparent that war was imminent, many of the Saudi and Arab officers were surprised that it began the day after the United Nations deadline had expired on 15 January. Others were faced with the reality that they had attacked another Arab state, that now Arabs were killing brother Arabs. This was not the fight that many felt they had trained and practiced for. Many had believed that if battles were to be fought in the Middle East, their antagonists would be either the Iranians or the Israelis. Arab disputes were not solved on the battlefield but at summit meetings. Of course, that particular myth had been shattered already by the Iraqi invasion of Kuwait five months earlier.

We all waited anxiously for the initial reports to come in from the CENTAF (U.S. Air Force, Central Command) command post in the Royal Saudi Air Force headquarters building. Surprisingly, all of the aircraft in the initial attacks on Baghdad returned to base safely. Original planning estimates of losses for the first night had been in the range of fifteen to twenty aircraft. Later that night, a U.S. Navy F/A-18 fighter aircraft was downed near the Syrian-Iraqi border. The next day, there were other losses, all to heavy antiaircraft fire and air defense missiles. It is believed that no coalition aircraft were lost due to air-to-air combat, although the reason for one shoot-down was never determined and may have been an Iraqi air-to-air victory. All in all, the air campaign had gotten off to a successful start—more successful than anyone had imagined.

Several air forces and services contributed combat aircraft to the coalition air campaign. In addition to aircraft from the U.S. Air Force and U.S. Navy, combat planes from the U.S. Marine Corps, the Royal Air Force (UK), the Royal Saudi Air Force (RSAF), and the Italian Air Force conducted offensive sorties into Iraq and Kuwait, operating from bases in Saudi Arabia, Bahrain, and the United Arab Emirates. Long-range B-52 bombers flew from bases in Spain, Diego Garcia in the southern Indian Ocean, and even the continental United States. The U.S. Navy was operating from six carriers, three in the Red Sea and three in the Persian Gulf. Canadian fighters performed defensive patrols over northern Saudi Arabia. French Air Force fighter aircraft participation in coalition flight operations was limited to Jaguar aircraft because the radar signature of French-piloted Mirage F-1 fighters would be identical to that of the French-built Mirages flown by the Iraqi Air Force.

Control, although not actual "command," of all this combat aviation and the hundreds of support flights—such as reconnaissance, command

and control, refueling tankers, resupply, and rescue—fell to the Joint
Forces Air Component Commander (JFACC). The JFACC, or "air boss,"
was the commander of CENTAF, Lt. Gen. Charles Horner. While U.S. Air
Force aircraft were under the direct command of the dual-hatted JFACC
and CENTAF commander, all other aircraft, both U.S. and coalition, were
placed under his centralized operational control; actual command of
these assets was retained by the parent services and countries. The
placement of these aircraft under the centralized operational control
of the JFACC—a U.S. Air Force officer—caused little problem among
the U.S. Navy and the coalition allies, who recognized that the U.S. Air
Force was providing the lion's share of air assets, both quantitatively as
well as qualitatively, to the campaign. However, relinquishing operational control of U.S. Marine Corps aviation assets to the JFACC was a
source of consternation among marine commanders. Since U.S. Army
aviation assets (almost exclusively helicopters) were retained opera-
tionally by their parent army commanders and not placed under the
control of the JFACC, the marines expected that their own aviation assets
(which included helicopters and fixed-wing aircraft) would also be
exempt from being placed under the operational control of the JFACC.
Marine air is considered an integral part of a marine division's organic
fire support—the firepower of its fighter and attack aircraft and its helicopter gunships offsetting its limited artillery capabilities.[2]

Every day the CENTAF staff published the Air Tasking Order (ATO),
a voluminous document that included every aircraft sortie for the next
day as well as ballistic and cruise missile attacks, since they would operate in the same airspace. When printed, the tasking order was thicker
than the New York City phone book. The biggest difficulty—the task of
getting the information to the aircraft wings, groups, squadrons, and
carriers—underscored a serious interoperability problem between the
U.S. Navy and the U.S. Air Force. Distribution of the ATO to air force
units was generally easy since they used the standard integrated U.S. Air
Force mission-planning system. However, transmitting the vast amount
of mission-planning data over already-crowded secure communications
circuits to U.S. Navy units not linked into the standard system proved
to be cumbersome and time-consuming. In fact, courier aircraft normally flew a printed copy of the ATO from Riyadh to the navy's carriers each day to ensure that the information needed to plan missions
arrived on time. This interoperability problem between the two U.S.

services was, in fact, highlighted after the war by congressional investigators. Coalition allies, who were generating only about 10 percent of the sorties, were provided hard copy of the information they needed.

One of the unspoken—and very sensitive—American goals in the early phase of the air war was to have a decisive and publicized Arab attack on Iraq. Most of the domestic American and much of the international news coverage focused on the U.S. role in the air war. Not much attention was being paid to the efforts of other members of the coalition. One could get the impression that the war was the United States versus Iraq rather than a coalition versus Iraq. The domestic Arab press had little to report to convince their populations that there was an Arab-versus-Arab angle to Desert Storm.

Along that line, during the first week of the war, planners had tasked the Saudi CSS-2 "East Wind" ballistic missile force to launch warheads at Iraqi targets. The Saudis had purchased the intermediate-range missiles from China in the late 1980s, knowing that the U.S. Congress would never approve the purchase of any type of American ballistic missile capable of reaching Israel. Congressional approval of the sale of any weapon system by the United States to Saudi Arabia (or to any Arab country) was subject to the intense pressure that could be applied by the powerful and highly effective Israeli lobby. However, the Saudis declined to launch their missiles. Although they did not give a reason, I suspect that either the system was not as capable as claimed or the Saudis were not yet proficient in operating the system.

By an interesting coincidence, the Saudi officer responsible for the acquisition of the Chinese missile system was Gen. Khalid bin Sultan, who at the time of the missile deal was commander of the Royal Saudi Air Defense Force. Khalid says in his book *Desert Warrior* that he ordered the missiles to be readied for launch but that the king never agreed to their use, wanting to prevent any innocent civilian casualties.[3] The Saudis were still concerned about the potential negative image of Arabs killing Arabs.

In the early days of the air war, when the Iraqi Air Force was still capable of launching sorties—before Saddam ordered the pilots to fly their aircraft to refuge in Iran and before many fighter aircraft were parked beside archeological treasures and antiquities—we got a second chance to force a Saudi-Iraqi engagement. On 24 January, there was an Iraqi attempt to mount an air attack into Saudi Arabia. It was obvious even during the attack that the primary goal of the strike was a psychological impact rather than a military one. Two Mirage F-1 fighters took off from one base in southern Iraq, followed shortly by two MiG-23 fighters from another base. They were detected and tracked from takeoff by U.S. Air Force AWACS radar planes over northern Saudi Arabia. The four aircraft joined up and headed south in formation. Because of documents and flight maps captured at the sector air operations center at Tallil Air Base near An-Nasiriyah after the war, we know that the Mirages were armed with incendiary bombs and were to attack the major Saudi oil refinery at Abqaiq, located just a few miles northwest of the port at Dhahran. Incendiary munitions detonating in the refinery and storage areas would cause a major conflagration. While a strike by two aircraft would not affect the outcome of the war, it would send a signal to the coalition that the Iraqis meant to fight and had the capability to mount air strikes of their own. The MiG-23 pilots were to provide fighter protection for the Mirages.

As the four aircraft flew south out of Iraq, the U.S. AWACS was told to clear the airspace ahead of the Iraqi fighters and vector a pair of Royal Saudi Air Force F-15 Eagle fighters against them. This order came from General Schwarzkopf, who wanted an Arab to engage an Iraqi, thus demonstrating that the ongoing combat operations were a multinational effort against Iraq and were not being conducted by the United States alone. A barrier patrol of U.S. Marine AV-8 Harriers and U.S. Air Force F-15 Eagles was placed behind the RSAF fighters in case the Iraqis got past the Saudis. At this time the intended target of the Iraqi aircraft was presumed (incorrectly) to be the port of Dhahran, a major entry point for U.S. troops and materiel. As soon as the pair of RSAF fighters turned toward the Iraqi formation and illuminated the aircraft with target acquisition radars, the pilots of the two MiG-23s, in a show of cowardice, broke off from the formation and dove for the deck. The MiGs returned to their base in Iraq, leaving the pilots of the bomb-laden Mirages with no fighter cover. Had the Mirage pilots turned as well, the engagement may well have been over at that point. However, they pressed on toward their target. The lead Saudi pilot, Capt. 'Iyad Al-Shamrani, rolled his F-15 behind the two now-maneuvering Mirages and downed both with air-to-air missiles, thus becoming the first pilot in RSAF history to shoot down two enemy aircraft. More importantly, a Saudi pilot had engaged (and defeated) Iraqi aircraft—an Arab-versus-Arab battle.

Soon after this engagement, the Iraqi military leadership in Baghdad realized the Iraqi Air Force could not fly and fight effectively against the coalition. The Iraqis decided it was better to try to attempt to relocate as many of their most modern fighters as possible outside of the country rather than lose them. Over one hundred twenty Iraqi Air Force aircraft, including many of its late-generation MiG-29 fighters, fled to Iran in hopes that an accommodation might be reached in the future and the aircraft returned to Iraq. Despite the later warming of relations, the Iraqi aircraft were either put into service with the Islamic Republic of Iran Air Force or were stripped for parts by the Iranians—or, as of 1998, are still sitting in Iranian storage facilities.

All members of the coalition did not universally laud the employment of American air power. One critic was the Kuwaiti government-in-exile, which received reports of damage caused by the air campaign from elements of the Kuwaiti resistance operating inside the occupied country. The Kuwaiti resistance consisted of several groups with the courage to fight the Iraqi occupation force, knowing that capture meant a gruesome death under torture. We received valuable intelligence reports from the Kuwaiti resistance via the exiled Kuwaiti government, which was set up in Taif, in southwestern Saudi Arabia. When the volume of these reports saturated the CIA's capabilities, the CENTCOM intelligence staff in Riyadh assisted in translating the reports. The resistance provided useful data on Iraqi troop dispositions in Kuwait as well as excellent information on Iraqi plans to torch the oil wells and on conditions in the capital city. As the air campaign shifted its focus to the south, concentrating on Iraqi troops in Kuwait in preparation for the ground assault, a massive amount of air power was applied to a relatively small area, with resultant high levels of damage to the Kuwaiti infrastructure. Iraqi troops had dug in around the oil wells because they believed that the oil fields—with derricks, pipelines, and wires—presented an obstacle to the mechanized and armored coalition forces and thus afforded the Iraqis some protection. Since the oil fields were where the Iraqis had put their troops, that is where U.S. pilots put their ordnance.

In late January, the Kuwaiti government-in-exile forwarded a letter to General Schwarzkopf along with a package of raw intelligence reports from the resistance inside Kuwait. Since the letter was in Arabic, it was given to me for translation. Included with the letter was a photocopy of a U.S. military nomenclature plate, the black and silver metal tag attached to all U.S. military equipment. The plate details such things as the name of the item, its specifications, its contract number, the contractor's name, and its date of manufacture. This particular plate identified a U.S. Navy cluster-bomb dispenser—basically a container filled with small bomblets used to attack armor formations or to disperse area denial munitions (small mines). When I translated the letter attached to the copy of the plate, I learned that the plate had been found in the Al-Burqan oil field, located in south-central Kuwait. The letter went on to complain that the U.S. and coalition air strikes were causing great damage to the very oil fields that would be necessary to generate revenue to rebuild Kuwait after the war. We were asked to stop such attacks. General Schwarzkopf dictated a reply expressing regret for the extensive damage to Kuwaiti industry but explaining that the Iraqis had taken up positions in these areas. Eventually coalition troops would have to clear these areas, and it was his duty to ensure that when the attack came, he had taken all possible actions to lessen coalition casualties. The Kuwaiti leadership stopped complaining but remained convinced that the air power applied in Kuwait was excessive.

On 25 January, the day after the attempted Iraqi air strike on Abqaiq, Iraqi forces in Kuwait opened the large pipelines connecting the Al-Ahmadi oil terminal to the offshore loading buoys, releasing two hundred thousand barrels of crude oil a day directly into the normally clear waters of the Persian Gulf. Their reason was never fully explained, but analysts assumed it was an effort to stymie coalition operations off the Kuwaiti coast. Others were of the opinion that the Iraqis were involved in "eco-terrorism," hoping that such heinous acts would cause the coalition to reassess its role in attacks against Iraq. The result of Iraq's action was a long oil slick moving south toward the desalinization plants on the Saudi coast, creating a direct threat to the kingdom's—and the coalition's—fresh water supply.

In addition to the water problem, CENTCOM analysts and Saudi Ministry of Petroleum and Mineral Resources engineers forecast ecological destruction on an unimaginable scale if the flow was not stopped. As it was, thousands of cormorants died, and marine life was devastated. Saddam Husayn's rape of Kuwait had now spread to the environment. The Kuwaiti resistance was able to provide the blueprints, obtained inside Kuwait, of the Al-Ahmadi oil terminal, allowing U.S. Air Force targeteers (target intelligence officers) to determine the best method to strike the terminal to stem the flow of crude oil hemorrhaging into the Gulf. Two F-111 fighter-bombers used laser-guided bombs to destroy the pumps and outlet manifolds and stopped the flow.

In late February, just prior to the initiation of the ground offensive, King Fahd asked for a situation update from General Schwarzkopf. The king was informed daily as to the status of the air campaign, usually by RSAF intelligence officers. Most of the information used in these briefings was extracted from CENTCOM directorate of intelligence briefings. This is not to say that the RSAF briefers couldn't produce the essential facts, but the CENTCOM daily briefing was a comprehensive product given in both English and Arabic, and it was already completed. The Saudi General Intelligence Directorate (GID, the Saudi equivalent of the CIA) also gave the king updates on their analysis of the situation. However, the GID primarily reported on what political events were likely to affect Saudi foreign policy and on what their agents abroad were hearing about the progress of the war. However, very little of the information could be considered hard intelligence concerning the effects of the air war on Iraq and Saddam Husayn. For that, the king wanted to hear the American military perspective from the general officer primarily responsible for prosecuting the war. Although it was usual for General Khalid zealously to attend any function that might give anyone the perception that Schwarzkopf had higher standing than he, the prince chose not to attend this particular briefing to his uncle.

General Schwarzkopf directed me to prepare a briefing in Arabic for King Fahd. Although he understood English to some degree, the monarch preferred to have all official conversations translated into Arabic to eliminate any potential misunderstandings. The general and I drove from the MODA building to the Al-Yamamah palace complex, where we waited for an audience with the king. We arrived shortly after 11:00 P.M. and were directed to the king's personal bunker deep under the palace. Being told the king might be available at 2:00 A.M., we were then ushered into a luxurious waiting room with multiple satellite television systems and an impressive offering of pastries and snacks.

The facility beneath the palace could hardly be called a bunker. Although it was fully hardened against bombs, it was an underground palace, with complete kitchen and living areas and a medical clinic. The entire facility, opulent beyond description, reminded me of the baroque palaces of old Europe. At about 2:30 A.M. we were shown the conference room, where the king would receive the briefing. The palace staff explained where the king would sit and how he preferred to run things. We had brought large briefing maps, but there were no stands—and not even room for stands. I indicated that I could brief from the top of the huge conference table, if that would be permitted. I had no idea how close one was allowed to be near the Saudi monarch. Surprisingly, I was told I could stand immediately next to the king so that I could point out places on the maps and photographs. I readied the materials, and we waited for the king.

The proper greeting for a king has always posed questions for American officials. Since the United States does not recognize royalty in its own right, monarchs are afforded the same courtesies as heads of state. American officials are not required to address foreign monarchs and members of royal families in the formal terms that are used in their particular countries. However, there is a separate protocol for addressing each level of royalty in Saudi Arabia: the king is usually referred to in English as "Your Majesty," while each member of the immediate Sa'ud family is referred to as "Your Royal Highness" and every member of the extended family as "Your Highness."

It was interesting to note the deference that senior military officers paid to members of the royal family who served in the armed forces at subordinate ranks. In the C3IC, we had a Saudi land-force captain who was a member of the immediate royal family. The name "Al Sa'ud" on his uniform assured deferential treatment by even Saudi generals, who addressed him as "Your Royal Highness." Some of the Saudi officers demanded that we use the Saudi form of address since the man was a prince. Our response was that he was not our prince. We Americans felt more comfortable using the military rank, and I believe the prince felt more at ease with that as well. When briefing the king, I chose to use the standard military "sir." The Saudi officials present assured me that this would not be construed as offensive.

The king entered the room for the briefing at about 3:15 A.M. I was impressed with his congeniality and warmth toward us. He shook hands with each of the officers in the party and asked us to sit down and begin. General Schwarzkopf began with a few words that the air campaign was progressing well and achieving the objectives. After the king's interpreter translated this, the general introduced me as the officer to give the situation briefing. I began with the customary Arabic Islamic greeting "As

Salam 'Alaykum" (peace be upon you), gave my name, and launched into my presentation. The king seemed to be slightly taken aback as I continued in Arabic. Smiling broadly and nodding at General Schwarzkopf, King Fahd exclaimed, "Huwa biyatakalam bal-'arabi. Mumtaz, mumtaz!" (He is speaking in Arabic. Excellent, excellent!). He appeared genuinely pleased that the U.S. leadership had been thoughtful enough to find an officer who could brief him in Arabic. The session went well. The king had only one question about a minor border skirmish near the town of 'Ar'ar, located far to the west of the planned ground-assault area.

The value of air power in general and during the Gulf War in particular has been hotly debated—and will be for years to come. The army and the marines claimed that the air campaign was "preparation of the battlefield." However, a sign over Dave Deptula's desk in the CENTAF command center summed up the air force position: "We are not preparing the battlefield—we are destroying it." Deptula, the author of the master attack plans for each day of the air campaign, suggests that the best judges of the impact of air power in the Gulf War are those Iraqis who were the targets of the air campaign. The debriefings of the tens of thousands of Iraqi prisoners indicate that the thousand-hour air campaign was far more decisive in determining the outcome of Desert Storm than the hundred-hour ground operation, which in the air force has come to be known as the "great prisoner roundup."

10

Of Scuds and Patriots

Faced both with the approaching United Nations 15 January deadline to accede to Security Council resolutions to leave Kuwait and with the certainty of American air strikes, Saddam Husayn again threatened to attack Israel in retaliation for any coalition action against Iraq. One could not easily forget that nine months earlier—in the spring of 1990—he threatened to "burn" Israel and claimed to have binary chemical weapons to back up that threat. We knew he had the chemical warheads, but we did not know if he would use them or any other of the chemical weapons he clearly had.

Most of the troops deployed to Saudi Arabia believed that Iraqi Scud missile attacks would be a virtual certainty, and they were prepared for it. Further, most analysts believed Saddam would probably launch a missile attack on Israel in an attempt to split the coalition. Many of these analysts, including me, also believed he would be successful if such an attack drew the expected Israeli military response. No Arab leader could survive the popular backlash if he became the tacit ally of Israel once the Israelis had attacked an Arab brother, even an Iraqi Arab brother who had invaded yet another Arab brother. This situation is most easily explained by the Arab proverb "Me against my brother; me and my brothers against our cousins; me, my brothers, and our cousins against the outsiders."

Almost twenty-four hours to the minute after the initial American air strikes on Baghdad, Saddam acted on his threat to strike Israel. At 3:03

A.M. on Friday, 18 January, Iraqi forces launched a salvo of five Al-Husayn missiles at Tel Aviv and Haifa from fixed launchers in western Iraq. Although the United States had quickly developed a system of providing missile-launch warnings to the Israelis using space-based sensors, the system was not in place for the first salvo. I was on duty that Friday night in the C3IC—which, despite its "coalition" name, was in reality the Saudi command post. We received the launch warning from the North American Aerospace Defense Command (NORAD) in Colorado Springs, whose satellites had detected the launches in western Iraq. Although the missiles' flight time to target was only about seven and a half to eight minutes, we knew within about ninety seconds of launch the trajectory of the missiles—they were headed for Israel. We knew, but the Israelis did not. We were watching CNN (via a satellite feed from the Armed Forces Radio and Television Service [AFRTS] facility in Italy), at that time coincidentally broadcasting a live segment from Tel Aviv in which unsuspecting Israelis on the streets were asked their opinions on the start of the Gulf War. All of us in the C3IC, Americans and Saudis alike, knew of the impending assault.

Two warheads impacted within seconds of each other, one explosion lighting up the TV screen. To the shock of the Americans present in the C3IC, virtually every Saudi officer was on his feet applauding and cheering the Iraqi missile strike against Israel, many shouting "Allahu akbar" (God is great). It was an awkward moment, watching Iraqi missiles striking a country not involved in this conflict. However, my assumption about Israel's lack of involvement in the conflict was faulty.

When I asked the Saudis why they were cheering an enemy attack, they described Israel as the greater enemy. When explained in Arabic, what they said makes much more sense than it does in English. The Saudis used the term "an enemy" (*'adu*) when describing the Iraqis, but they added the definite article "the" when describing the Israelis—"the enemy" (*al-'adu*). In Arabic context, this has a greater magnitude, is much a stronger statement, than the use of the word without the definite article. One of the senior Saudi officers explained that the Iraqi "situation" was not nearly as grave or important as the overarching Israeli "issue." He said that if the Israelis were to retaliate against Iraq, the Saudis and other Arab countries in the coalition—Egypt, Syria, Morocco, the Gulf states, and so on—would stop fighting Iraq and join forces with Saddam to defeat (or attempt to defeat) the Israelis. After that was done, they would work out the lesser "internal" problem with the Iraqis. After all, as the Arabs say, "the enemy of my enemy is my friend."

As it turned out, the Iraqis used only conventional warheads against Israel, and Israel acceded to American pressure to remain outside the conflict. Israeli intervention would in all likelihood have fractured the coalition—exactly what Saddam was counting on. I believe that if the Al-Husayn missiles that struck Israel had been equipped with chemical warheads, no amount of American arm-twisting would have prevented an overwhelming Israeli military response. Although Saddam may have thought he had created a strategic deterrent against Israel with the construction of missile launch complexes in western Iraq—missiles capable of carrying chemical agent warheads—an attack on Tel Aviv using chemical weapons would have probably triggered an Israeli nuclear strike on Iraq.

Several of the senior Saudi officers attempted to play down the concern of the American (as well as British and French) officers present at that moment. Every time there were missile attacks on Israel, the atmosphere in the C3IC got very tense. The Saudis wanted to applaud and cheer. After all, here was an Arab leader successfully striking the enemy they had been conditioned to hate from birth—an enemy that had consistently humiliated Arabs on the battlefield and that now appeared impotent before Saddam Husayn, who likened himself to Saladin (Salah Al-Din Al-Ayyubi), the Muslim liberator of Jerusalem from the control of the Crusaders in 1187. But the Arabs now considered Jerusalem an occupied city, with the Al-Aqsa mosque—the third holiest shrine in Islam—and the Dome of the Rock mosque under "Zionist" (Israeli) control. Although many Arabs like to cite Saladin's exploits, he was not an Arab but a Kurd—the same people who had been the targets of Iraqi chemical weapons attacks in 1988. The tension in the C3IC never went away completely.

At the same time missiles were launched at Israel, in Saudi Arabia a salvo was fired at Dhahran, and the next night four missiles were launched into Riyadh. Unlike the Israelis, American troops in Riyadh and Dhahran lived under the protection of an umbrella of U.S. Army Patriot air defense missiles. The success or failure of the Patriot system against Iraq's Al-Husayn and Al-'Abbas missiles has been the subject of numerous studies, debates, and statistical analyses. For those of us who went through the attacks in Saudi Arabia, the system was a success.

The first missile attack on Riyadh came shortly after midnight on 19 January. The initial indication was the air-raid sirens most of us had not heard since grade school in the 1950s, when we crouched under our desks to protect ourselves against simulated Soviet nuclear strikes. As in Tel Aviv, no one knew what types of warheads were carried by the missiles, so we were told to assume the worst. That meant a chemical or biological agent warhead. My roommates (eleven of us shared a two-bedroom apartment—which was better than living in a tent) and I donned gas masks and helmets and gathered in the hallway of our building, which appeared to be the safest place.

Our immediate concern was protection from the actual strike of a missile—the high-energy impact of a large object slamming into the earth at an incredible velocity. Secondly, there was the warhead to consider—was it high-explosive, chemical, or biological? Although we should have been more concerned with the impact and high-explosive warheads, the thought of a nerve gas or anthrax attack was unsettling. We at least had been trained in chemical-warfare defense and had gas masks and appropriate pharmaceuticals. As far as a warhead filled with anthrax spores was concerned, most of the Americans assigned to units that were the likely targets of a biological attack (primarily headquarters units) had been vaccinated against the disease in the months leading to the war. The fact that we had been vaccinated was classified at the time because there was not enough of the vaccine to inoculate all the Americans, let alone other members of the coalition.[1]

While the air-raid siren was going off, I made a phone call to the C3IC. I was told, "Four, coming our way"—four missiles were inbound to Riyadh (as opposed to Dhahran). After NORAD detection of a launch, it took two or three minutes for the air-raid sirens in Riyadh to be activated. Since the Al-Husayn or Al-'Abbas missiles' flight time from launch to impact is between seven and eight minutes, we normally had only about four minutes of warning. Almost exactly four minutes after the sirens started going off, there were several series of sharp and booming explosions, many more than the four missile impacts we had expected. What we were hearing, but did not realize at that time, were Patriot air defense missiles leaving their launchers. A Patriot missile is about fifteen feet long and is launched from an enclosed tube. By the time the missile has cleared its launch tube, it is already traveling to the target at supersonic speeds. Launching a missile from zero almost instantly to supersonic velocity requires thrust that amounts to a controlled explosion. Our apartment building was located about half a mile from a Patriot battery, so we could feel the concussions from the launches as well as see the streaks of light as the missiles climbed to meet the incoming Scud warheads. Successful Patriot intercepts resulted in an awesome fireworks display of light, explosions, and burning debris falling to earth. We quickly learned to tell the differences among Patriot launches, aerial intercepts of Scuds by the Patriots, and Scud impacts.

During the buildup of forces in Desert Shield, one of the critical procurement actions was the acquisition of as many Patriot missiles with the tactical ballistic missile interceptor fuze called the Patriot Advanced Capability-2 (PAC-2) as the manufacturer, Raytheon, could produce. There were few in the inventory.

The Patriot was originally designed to intercept fast-moving aircraft, not inbound ballistic missiles. Raytheon engineers and army air defense officers were able to develop new system software and modified fuzes to handle the faster speed of ballistic missiles. In one of the first engagements against seven Scuds, Patriot batteries fired thirty-seven of the scarce PAC-2-fuzed missiles. General Schwarzkopf told his staff we could not afford to fire that many missiles at so few Scuds and asked them why so many Patriots were being launched. The senior air defense officer explained that the radar systems were set to automatically engage any detected inbound warheads because manually engaging the targets would require humanly impossible precision and high-speed calculations. If the Patriot system had fired two missiles at each inbound Scud warhead as the computer had been programmed to do, only fourteen interceptors, not thirty-seven, should have engaged seven Scuds. The officer had no explanation for why so many Patriots were launched.

Analysis of Scud debris showed that the modified Scuds being launched by Iraq were exiting the atmosphere because of their lighter weight, whereas a normal Scud remained in the atmosphere throughout its entire flight. Iraqi modifications to the Scuds included a reduced warhead weight and a higher fuel load, combined with adjustments that caused the liquid fuel to be burned in the early stages of the flight trajectory. As the fuel in the tanks, which were located between the heavy rocket motor and the relatively heavy warhead, burned off faster than designed in the normal Scud, the missiles became unstable in the upper atmosphere, their flight path now unpredictable and their accuracy reduced.[2]

The instability resulting from these modifications was causing the missiles to break up during exit from and reentry into the atmosphere. The Patriot radars, tracking all of the pieces as they broke up, assigned two missiles to intercept each piece large enough to be a warhead. After some adjustments to the Patriot radar software were made, fewer interceptors were launched.

In February, surveillance radar at a NATO air base in Turkey used by the U.S. Air Force to conduct air strikes against Iraq appeared to have detected an inbound Scud. In response to the threat, the U.S. Army Patriot battery set up to protect the base launched a missile. The Patriot was command-detonated after the target was determined to be an anomaly in the radar set and not an actual Scud attack.

A CNN reporter covering the story ridiculed the Patriot battery for launching the missile against a suspected target, stating that "at one million dollars a copy, one would think they would be sure of the target before launching such an expensive weapon." I wrote a letter, which still goes unanswered, to CNN chairman Ted Turner, inviting his reporter to come live with us in Riyadh. After a few multiple-missile Scud attacks with nine or ten jarring explosions overhead, the CNN reporter would have come to appreciate the protective umbrella provided by the Patriots and might, therefore, be less concerned about the costs of the hardware.

After the Scud attacks had become routine—as routine as a ballistic missile attack can be—and the Patriot system appeared to be defeating most of them, we usually took only minimum precautions. As Scud attacks became news events in the States, we were able to watch the strikes on television in our apartment, almost live. CNN placed a camera on one of the highest buildings in Riyadh, aimed north toward Iraq. When Scud launches were detected, the alarms were sounded within two or three minutes. The cameras were activated, and live news feeds began. The signal went back to Atlanta via satellite and was then broadcast to the world. Since Saudi Arabia censors television in the kingdom, CNN was rarely broadcast live over Saudi-controlled television. However, the AFRTS network carried CNN live throughout almost the entire war. These broadcasts were sent via satellite from the AFRTS facility in Italy to Riyadh and then cabled to the MODA bunker and U.S. housing areas. What we were watching was a split-second behind real time after three satellite relays from Riyadh to Atlanta to Italy to Riyadh. The sounds we were hearing directly over our heads, however, were live. Sometimes we went outside and watched the battle in the sky. At certain moments the display seemed almost like a video game; at other times it was very real. Some of the warheads got through and slammed into the ground, but fortunately, most of them impacted outside the populated areas of the city.

The Saudis were impressed with the performance of the Patriot system. General Khalid jokingly asked Schwarzkopf one day after a briefing on a Scud-Patriot engagement if Schwarzkopf thought that he should buy the company. Although Khalid was joking in this instance, he made a lot of money on the war. Many of the transportation contracts and food service contracts were let to companies owned or partially owned by Khalid. There were rumors that his personal gain of ten million dollars during the war was the main reason he was fired from the Saudi armed forces after the war.

The Iraqis launched a total of eighty-eight missiles, all but one at Israel or Saudi Arabia (one was fired ineffectively at Bahrain). Although Riyadh fared well through the Scud attacks, this was not the case in Dhahran. Because of the CENTCOM requirement to have overlapping radar coverage of areas housing American troops, many of the radars had to be kept operating longer between maintenance shutdowns than they had been designed to do. Close to the end of the war, during a period of time when one of the Patriot radars experienced a software malfunction because it had been on line too long, a Scud warhead struck a barracks full of American soldiers, killing twenty-eight and wounding ninety-eight.

Put in perspective, the Scud was a resource-draining weapon. Seven U.S. Air Force F-16 fighter sorties could deliver the entire tonnage of all Iraqi Scud missiles fired during the war. Yet hundreds of coalition air sorties were allocated to attempt to stop the launch of the missiles.

11

Bob Simon
Finds the War

THE BATTLE OF AL-KHAFJI

Realizing the devastation being wrought on Iraq by the U.S.-led air campaign, Saddam sought a means to force the initiation of the awaited ground campaign. The Iraqi leader knew he could not hold out indefinitely against the massive air power destroying his infrastructure and reasoned he would fare better against the coalition in a battle on the ground. He ordered his military commanders to launch an attack against the coalition in hopes it would be the catalyst for the ground campaign.

The Iraqi attack on the vacated northern Saudi city of Al-Khafji began with a mechanized assault in the early-morning hours of 30 January, two weeks after the beginning of Desert Storm. The Iraqi 15th Mechanized Infantry Brigade of the 5th Mechanized Infantry Division took the unprotected city just south of the Kuwait border, virtually without a fight. This bold attack into Saudi Arabia not only came as a shock to the American commanders but also represented a severe challenge to the Saudis—their first test in combat against the feared Iraqi army.

The initial reaction of the Saudi leadership was horror that a piece of Saudi Arabia was now occupied by Iraqi troops. King Fahd ordered the commander of Joint Forces, General Khalid, either to eject the Iraqis from Saudi territory or to have the Americans do it—immediately. Khalid's notion was to shift assets from the air campaign in Iraq to air strikes on Iraqi forces in Al-Khafji. Khalid suggested to General

119

Schwarzkopf that the U.S. Air Force eliminate the problem (and most of the city) through heavy bombardment by B-52 bombers. General Schwarzkopf counseled against this idea, and in the end it was decided that Arab forces would attempt to liberate the city. Schwarzkopf wanted Arab forces to engage in combat with the Iraqis for two basic reasons: to have the Saudis overcome their hesitation to fight other Arabs and to give the Saudis a success in order to bolster their confidence. A complicating factor for any plan to retake Al-Khafji was that two U.S. Marine Corps ground reconnaissance teams were in the city—their presence as yet unknown to the Iraqis.

The marine reconnaissance teams that had been trapped in the city during the Iraqi attack had now barricaded themselves in an apartment building to make their stand; they had nowhere else to go. Once the Iraqis discovered the presence of Americans, the Iraqi troops moved in. One of the objectives of the incursion into Saudi Arabia was to take American prisoners. Although the Iraqis seized the bottom floors, the marines' tenacious defense of their positions on the upper floors and the roof finally forced the Iraqis merely to surround the building and cease attempts to dislodge the young Americans. The marines' actions at Al-Khafji were relayed word-of-month to other Iraqi troops and reinforced the marines' reputation of ferocity in combat. Our interrogations of Iraqi prisoners yielded wild stories about the marines—that each marine had to have killed a member of his own family as a condition of entering the corps, that marines practiced cannibalism on the bodies of their foes, and so forth.

The Iraqis repulsed the initial assault by a Saudi infantry unit into the captured city. The second try to dislodge the Iraqis was heavily supported by U.S. Marine fighter aircraft and helicopter gunships anxious to protect their fellow marines trapped in the city. After the Iraqis began a withdrawal to better defense positions in the city, marine air liaison officers moving into the city were horrified to see Saudi soldiers looting from the dead Iraqi troops rather than consolidating their gains and preparing for a possible Iraqi counterattack. After senior Saudi officers arrived and observed the situation, order was restored, and the Saudis secured the routes into the city for follow-on forces.

In the end, a Qatari army tank unit supported by Saudi infantry liberated the city, again heavily covered by U.S. Marine and Air Force air power. The medium tanks used by the Qataris in the liberation of the city had been manufactured in France. Within days after the completion of the fighting, the French defense attaché office in Riyadh published a slick color brochure claiming the superiority of French weapons, citing their success at Al-Khafji. We pointed out to the French liaison officers in the MODA building that the brochure failed to include the range of weapons France had sold to the Iraqis. These included Mirage F-1 fighter aircraft, Exocet antiship missiles, ATLIS (automatic tracking laser illumination system) target designators, the Kari air defense system, and the French GCT (grande cadence de tir) self-propelled artillery system— all of which had been used in the invasion of Kuwait and were now arrayed against the coalition.[1]

After the battle, General Khalid flew to Al-Khafji to review the performance of his troops and to inspect the battle damage. Although Al-Khafji was a minor battle in the war, it was significant because it took place on Saudi soil and proved to the Saudis and other Arab coalition members that they could fight other Arabs and could defeat the Iraqis in combat.

THE BOB SIMON CONNECTION
Immediately following the seizure of Al-Khafji by Iraqi forces on 30 January, the Iraqi III Corps commander, Lt. Gen. Salah 'Abbud Mahmud Al-Daghastani, had ordered two additional brigades of other III Corps divisions—the 26th Armored and the 20th Mechanized Infantry Brigades—to move toward the city. These follow-on forces were to consolidate Iraqi gains, reinforce the 15th Brigade, which was already in the city, and prepare to repel the inevitable coalition counterattack. These forces were to move from their positions in Kuwait about forty miles to the west of the coastal road and advance southeasterly through Saudi Arabia toward Al-Khafji. The advance was stopped in its tracks by U.S. Air Force, Marine, and Navy fighter aircraft. The Iraqi units never reached the city.

The movement of the 26th Brigade into Saudi Arabia, which had been planned for some time, was key to Iraq's capitalizing on its thrust into Al-Khafji. In fact, the route of march from the brigade's positions in southern Kuwait to Al-Khafji had been thoroughly reconnoitered days earlier. However, we did not know of this reconnaissance effort until long after the smoke had cleared and Al-Khafji was back in coalition hands.

Later we were able to piece together from our interrogations of Iraqi prisoners of war a picture of the Iraqi reconnaissance operations prior to the battle of Al-Khafji. At around eleven o'clock on a moonless night in late January, a five-man Iraqi reconnaissance patrol had slipped over the Kuwaiti border into Saudi Arabia. The team was to determine a suitable route for the 26th Brigade to move into Al-Khafji when ordered to do so. As the team cleared the berm on the Saudi border, they had found themselves facing a surprised group of four men in a Chevrolet Caprice sedan. Unwittingly, CBS newsman Bob Simon had found the war.

Journalists during operations Desert Shield and Desert Storm faced many restrictions on their movements—constraints imposed for operational security as well as for the journalists' own personal safety. Normally, these individuals were required to have military escorts. Occasionally, however, one or two of them would set out on their own for a particular story, despite the rules. During one such excursion Bob Simon was attempting to get as close to the Kuwaiti border—the Iraqi front lines—as possible. He was in the company of three others, at least one of them a fellow American.

We determined later that Bob Simon had been captured by that Iraqi reconnaissance patrol from the 26th Armored Brigade. However, at the time, all we knew was that Simon and his team were missing. When they failed to return from their trip, a search was mounted. Shortly thereafter, their car was found empty, except for some expensive camera equipment. There were no signs of a struggle, no signs of injuries, and no bodies. Had they been killed by Bedouins, or captured by Iraqis, or had they sneaked into Kuwait on foot in search of a story?

About two weeks after the battle of Al-Khafji, I was on duty in the C3IC. The C3IC served not only as the liaison between U.S. and Joint Forces Command units but also as the main Saudi armed forces command post. Not satisfied with the volume and quality of reporting we were getting from Saudi military intelligence based on their interrogations of Iraqi deserters and prisoners, we had asked that the Saudis forward to us daily by fax the raw, handwritten field interrogation reports. We had provided a standard questionnaire to be used with all captured Iraqi troops. I noticed that while the Saudi interrogators generally followed the questionnaire, they did not follow up on affirmative answers. For example, if a question like "Do you know of plans for future attacks on coalition positions?" was answered with a "yes," the response was noted simply as such, with no amplification as to where, when, who, and so forth.

As I scanned the day's sheets of faxed hand-written Arabic questionnaires, something caught my eye. An Iraqi prisoner, a noncommissioned officer, had responded to a question about coalition prisoners by claiming that he had captured a team of American journalists in late January—about the twenty-sixth, as he remembered. No information followed that statement. There was no clarification, just that one entry. The report was in stack of about fifty other reports. But the reference to a team of American journalists could not be overlooked or ignored; after all, the news broadcasts were flooded with the story of Bob Simon's disappearance. I pointed out the report to the C3IC shift commander, the well-respected Saudi infantry officer Brig. Gen. 'Abd Al-Rahman Al-Marshad, and asked if he could find out which unit had interrogated the prisoner and sent in the report. He told me the report had originated from an element of the Royal Saudi Land Force 8th Mechanized Brigade, then occupying defensive positions on the Kuwaiti border. I asked Brigadier General Al-Marshad, with whom I had developed a close professional relationship, to have the brigade locate the prisoner and bring him to Riyadh immediately.

I met the prisoner the next day at a special detention area on the outskirts of Riyadh set up to handle high-ranking and special prisoners. By this time, we had obtained detailed information from CBS not only on Simon's car, clothing, and equipment but also on the three colleagues with whom he had last been seen. The Iraqi prisoner appeared confused that he was the center of such attention. I asked him to tell me why he thought the men he claimed to have captured were journalists. He described Simon's camera equipment accurately. I asked why he thought they were Americans. He said he initially believed they were Americans because they were wearing "American cowboy" trousers—which, after a few descriptive phrases, I understood to be jeans. More importantly, he told me he had asked the men who they were and they had replied that they were journalists from an American news network. Finally, he told me that he had checked their passports: two of them were American.

The Iraqi sergeant went on to explain that he was a member of a patrol of five soldiers who had carefully crawled through the Iraqi lines and obstacle belts and then across the Kuwaiti border and over the berm that had been erected on the Saudi side. Upon clearing the berm, they had immediately come upon a dark sedan with four occupants. The mission of the five Iraqis had been to find a suitable route of march for the 26th Brigade to move southeast (he had not known at the time that the route was to be used for a supporting attack after the 15th Brigade's assault on Al-Khafji, which was set to kick off in a few days). The team had not been looking for prisoners—in fact they were under orders to avoid enemy contact of any kind in order not to alert the coalition to Iraqi interest in the area or to impending offensive operations. With this in mind, the Iraqi sergeant had decided to take the news team into custody, escorting them back into Kuwait and turning them over to the brigade intelligence officer. From there, he was told, the news team had been immediately moved to Al-Basrah and then on to Baghdad, where they were to have been turned over to the Iraqi Intelligence Service, the Mukhabarat.

The information provided by the young prisoner coincided almost exactly with what we knew of the time and place of Simon's disappearance. The sedan was found exactly as the prisoner had described it—doors open and cameras inside. His description of the team's clothing matched with what we had been told by CBS. I notified the CENTCOM director of intelligence, Brig. Gen. Jack Leide, that we had fairly reliable information on the whereabouts of Bob Simon. We immediately briefed General Schwarzkopf, who called the president of CBS News to inform him that we had reason to believe that Bob Simon was alive, albeit a prisoner of the Iraqis. Since it was well known that Simon is Jewish and might be falsely accused of being a spy for Israel, CBS went public with the fact that they had been told by "Department of Defense sources" that their reporter was alive and being held prisoner in Baghdad. This international announcement put the Iraqis on notice that Simon's predicament was no secret and that they would be held accountable for his safety. We may never know what plans the IIS had for Simon or what, if any, difference the public announcement had made. He was later released unharmed.

I met Mr. Simon three years later in Damascus, Syria, while he was covering the visit of President Clinton and I was serving as the air attaché at the U.S. embassy. I explained how we had "found" him, but I asked that he not use the account in a news story. True to his word, he never has.

12

The Ground Assault

The decision to launch the long-awaited ground campaign was agonized over for days, even weeks. Coalition air forces had been systematically striking targets all over Iraq, and the focus was shifting to the south to destroy the Iraqi forces in the Kuwait Theater of Operations (KTO). Various factors had to be taken into consideration before the launching of almost five corps of ground troops into combat. In addition to normal planning factors such as the weather, the logistics, and the readiness of coalition forces, the primary considerations were the condition of the opposing Iraqi forces and the need, partially military and partially parochial, to engage the Iraqis on the ground.

To determine the timing of the ground attack, General Schwarzkopf and the other coalition commanders had to know the condition of the enemy forces. The whole question of bomb damage assessment (BDA) was highly controversial and misunderstood. Throughout the air campaign, it was necessary to quantify the success or failure of the strikes on the targets. When we were dealing with large "strategic" targets in Baghdad or other areas of Iraq, assessment of damage was important for us to be able to determine if the desired effects on Iraqi forces had been achieved. For example, whether or not strikes on command and control facilities had been successful determined whether or not the target had to be struck again. If the command and control facility, say for an air defense sector, was still operational, then U.S. and coalition aircraft operating in that sector were vulnerable to the air defense system.

125

Targets that could be repaired easily were automatically placed on the restrike list every few days to ensure they remained out of action.

The biggest problem with assessing actual damage to facilities and structures resulted from the different effects of the newer generation of munitions being used. Although precision guided munitions (PGM) had been employed before Desert Storm, they had never been utilized on this scale. Virtually every strike against targets in central Baghdad was conducted with PGMs. One reason was their accuracy and effectiveness, which minimized the need for pilots to revisit high-threat areas and also limited civilian casualties and collateral damage.

For the first time, the U.S. Air Force unveiled and used its heretofore secret "bunker buster" PGMs to strike hardened targets. When these PGMs struck a target, they penetrated the facility's concrete and armor outer structure, detonating deep inside. Gun camera footage—often released as part of CENTCOM's press briefings—showed the bunkers and buildings being struck and debris being blown out of doors and vents. Obviously a detonation had occurred deep inside the facility. However, it was difficult to assess the damage. Often the comparably small impact point was not visible to reconnaissance cameras because of look angles, weather, or other factors. A facility might appear to be normal in a photograph taken after a PGM strike, when actually the entire inside of the structure had been destroyed.

Iraq sheltered almost all of its combat aircraft in modern Yugoslav-made hardened aircraft shelters (HAS), built to exceed NATO standards. The PGMs punched small holes in the HAS exteriors and exploded inside the shelter, creating a contained explosion. In this case, it could be assumed that what was inside was destroyed. There were reports that Iraq had stored Scud missile launchers in HASs at Kuwait's 'Ali Al-Salim Air Base. These were targeted for strikes with PGMs. Although we could never be certain, the resulting explosions that literally ripped apart several of the HASs indicated that something with very volatile propellant, similar to liquid rocket fuel, had been stored in the shelter. Senior NATO officers expressed anger that they had not known the U.S. Air Force—in essence keeping secrets from close allies—possessed the capability to penetrate NATO's bunkers and HASs with almost unerring accuracy and devastating effect.

The same problem came into play in the effort to assess damage to Iraqi ground forces and associated military equipment. Often, in aerial reconnaissance or satellite photographs, destroyed tanks appeared to be operational. On one hand, tanks hit by laser-guided bombs normally were visibly destroyed or damaged. On the other hand, tanks that had been struck by depleted uranium rounds fired by the 30-mm Gatling gun on the A-10 often had only a few holes the size of a quarter, yet the tanks' interiors (and crews) had been completely destroyed.

Damage to Iraqi artillery pieces—key targets prior to the launch of the ground offensive—posed a difficult assessment problem. Damage to small components could render a gun useless, but such damage was almost impossible to detect from aerial or satellite photography. The standing orders from General Leide were to err on the side of caution. Unless something was clearly damaged, it was considered operational.

While it was useful methodology to count individual tanks, armored personnel carriers, field guns, and other equipment that had been destroyed, the real challenge came in the attempt to estimate the remaining combat effectiveness of Iraqi combat units deployed to the KTO. These were the units that U.S. and coalition forces would face when they launched their attacks into Kuwait and Iraq.

Schwarzkopf had stated that he wanted coalition air forces to reduce Iraqi combat capability by 50 percent before he gave the order to begin the ground offensive. Did that mean the destruction of half the tanks and artillery in the KTO? Destruction of equipment and combat effectiveness were not the same thing. Units could be combat effective with their equipment greatly reduced in quantity, or they could be ineffective and still have almost all of their equipment. Schwarzkopf tasked the director of intelligence to come up with a system of displaying combat effectiveness of Iraqi units on a map rather than merely counting numbers. Back in Washington, General Powell criticized the DIA's initial damage assessments, stating that he wanted to see intelligence analysis of residual Iraqi capabilities and not simply to look at anecdotal evidence and photographs.

Creating what was to become an extremely useful tool, army colonel (now major general) Chuck Thomas and a small select team of intelligence analysts came up with a color code to be applied to each Iraqi division's symbol on the map. Red meant an enemy unit was combat effective, yellow meant it was marginally effective, and green meant a unit had been rendered ineffective. Pockets of red could be singled out for increased air and artillery raids to bring the units' effectiveness down to an acceptable level. How were the colors assigned? In the absence of other data, a mathematical formula was used. For example, Iraqi infantry divisions included a tank battalion as an integral part of the unit. If that tank battalion was destroyed and a certain percentage of the division's artillery damaged, then the unit was considered combat ineffective against the mobility and heavy firepower of the U.S. and coalition divisions.

As it turned out, Thomas's system accurately portrayed the condition of Iraqi forces. However, BDA will continue to be a problem for the foreseeable future. Advanced weapons, whose effects are hard to detect with existing reconnaissance sensors, will be used more and more. Newer weapons and forms of warfare, such as information warfare, will make assessing the effects even more difficult.

Probably just as important as our knowing the condition of the forces arrayed against the coalition was knowing just who was out there. One of the key tasks of the intelligence community was to produce an accurate picture of the Iraqi forces—the "ground order of battle." That task was being accomplished through analysis of all-source information at CENTCOM, the DIA, and the CIA. Each intelligence organization's ground order of battle for the Iraqi forces in the KTO differed. The closest in agreement were those of CENTCOM and the DIA. There were daily, sometimes hourly, consultations between CENTCOM's military analysts in Riyadh and the DIA's military analysts in Washington. The CIA preferred to produce its assessments independently. The levels of military expertise at CENTCOM and the DIA were comparable; the DIA was made up of military officers and Defense Department civilian employees, most with some military experience.

On the other hand, CIA analysts were almost exclusively civilians, most having little or no military experience. The majority of those who did have this kind of experience had served at lower levels (company, battalion, squadron, and wing) and were unfamiliar with operations at corps level or higher. Unfortunately, this lack of military experience is now becoming the norm rather than the exception across the intelligence community as a whole, including the intelligence organizations of the Defense Department. With the end of the draft in the 1970s, fewer people are now serving in the armed forces, and the number of civilian intelligence analysts with military experience is declining. Despite efforts by the intelligence agencies to provide ancillary training to replicate this experience, it is not the same as actually serving in a military unit. This lack of military experience among analysts in the intelligence community is exacerbated by the fact that the military services, all downsizing in the wake of the end of the Cold War, are reluctant to provide their best intelligence officers to the national agencies. As a result, the quality of those agencies' military analysis will continue to decline.

As the launch of the ground offensive drew closer, the focus of the air campaign incrementally shifted from targets all over Iraq and concentrated on Iraqi ground forces in the KTO. One of the coincidental benefits of the increased air attacks on the units in the regions where the ground war would be fought was the destruction of much of the landline communications between Iraqi military units. This was complemented by the insertion of special forces teams into Kuwait and southern Iraq to destroy communications facilities, primarily landlines. As these primary communications nets were disrupted, the Iraqi units were forced to communicate over microwave and other radio nets. These radio transmissions were all vulnerable to collection by U.S. intercept sites and reconnaissance platforms.

Another intelligence benefit in shifting the air strikes to the KTO was the huge increase in the number of deserters flooding across the Iraqi lines to surrender to coalition forces. Each of these deserters was a potential source of information. Iraqi deserters and prisoners of war, for the most part, were cooperative when interrogated. Unlike American servicemembers, who are trained to resist interrogations, most Iraqi soldiers appeared willing to provide information to their coalition interrogators. Perhaps their cooperation was a result of the humane treatment and steady food rations they received from their captors. As American officers, we were appalled at the conditions in many of the Iraqi units. The first duty of an officer in any military is to take care of his or her troops. Iraq's utter failure in this regard was probably the key factor in the collapse of Iraqi morale.

One aspect of the handling of Iraqi deserters and prisoners was troublesome. Prior to the start of the war, the Saudis were responsible for handling and interrogating defectors and deserters. After the war had begun, these Iraqis were no longer defectors but prisoners of war, and at this point, the capturing unit became responsible for them. When the initial Iraqi deserters arrived in northern Saudi Arabia, the Saudis declared that they, as brother Arabs, would take charge. Any questions American intelligence had for the deserters was to be sent through the Saudis. We objected strongly, and finally we were granted direct access to the Iraqis.

One of the things we wanted to do was to take blood samples from Iraqi prisoners for testing to determine if the Iraqis had been vaccinated for anthrax or had been treated with chemical warfare defense medicines. If either of these tests were positive, it would indicate Iraqi preparedness or intent to use chemical or biological weapons—we already knew their willingness and capability.

The Saudis initially refused to allow us to draw blood from their brother Muslims. I suggested we draw blood from Iraqi Christians, some of whom had agreed to give blood when we asked. Still, the Saudis refused. It took the personal intervention of General Leide to overturn the Saudi refusal. The tests were negative. The results indicated that the Iraqis had not been vaccinated for protection against biological agents or administered any prophylactic chemical warfare medicines.

As the tempo of the bombings of troop formations and frontline units increased, the flood of deserters increased. Statistically the most effective aircraft used during the war was the F-117 Nighthawk stealth fighter, and accordingly it received most of the publicity in the Western media. However, to the average Iraqi soldier in the trenches of Kuwait and southern Iraq, the most feared plane in the world was the legendary B-52. These heavy bombers, which normally struck targets while in a three-ship formation, would form into squadrons of nine to twelve aircraft and drop almost half a million pounds of high-explosive ordnance on a particular Iraqi division, sometimes twice on the same division in one day.

Psychological operations targeted other divisions with leaflets warning that the B-52 bombers were coming for them another day. Normally, desertions increased dramatically after a neighboring unit was hit with a massed B-52 raid. I once interrogated an Iraqi prisoner who claimed to have deserted because of the B-52 air raids. I asked what unit he was from. When he told me the 20th Infantry Division, I was puzzled because the 20th had not been bombed yet. He explained that he had watched a B-52 raid on the neighboring division and did not want to undergo similar bombardment. From the coalition front lines, you could normally see the B-52s headed north and then turn onto an easterly or westerly course to begin their bomb run. It looked ominous from where we were. One can only imagine the sense of dread felt by the Iraqis as the B-52s approached, the sense of relief if the planes continued on their way, and the terrifying fear if they didn't. The ground tremors from the bomb detonations could be felt miles away.

The B-52 raids were combined with F-111 fighter-bombers conducting precision strikes in a tactic that came to be known as "tank plinking" —using laser-guided bombs to hit individual pieces of armor and artillery. One F-111 with six laser-guided bombs meant six tanks destroyed. Six aircraft could effectively destroy (or render ineffective) an Iraqi tank battalion in one mission. The Iraqi troops faced a quandary: stay in armored vehicles and be hit with laser-guided bombs or stay outside the vehicles and hope the B-52s were headed elsewhere.

After reviewing the new information derived from the increased radio traffic intercepts and the reports from the interrogations of the new wave of deserters, CENTCOM intelligence analysts noted major discrepancies in the Iraqi ground order of battle as carried by CENTCOM, the DIA, and the CIA. While we were rather certain of the number and location of armored vehicles and artillery pieces, and had a good estimate of the number of Iraqi troops in the KTO, we were less sure of the unit designators of the formations. Through satellite and aerial photography, we had an accurate picture of the units facing coalition forces, but photography cannot usually reveal a unit's identity.[1] For example, we knew from photography that there was an Iraqi infantry division immediately ahead of the Saudi 8th Brigade. Though we were calling it the 20th Infantry Division, we were not sure that was correct.

As more information became available in the days leading up to the launch of the ground offensive, we grew less and less confident in the accuracy of the designators we had assigned to Iraqi units. A small group of CENTCOM analysts—U.S. Army order of battle technicians and a Canadian Forces intelligence service captain assigned to the CENTCOM directorate of intelligence—came up with a complete new Iraqi order of battle based almost exclusively on the interrogation reports from the deserters and prisoners. While it did not change the number of units, strengths, or locations, it did rename well over half of the frontline units facing the coalition forces.

The senior CENTCOM analyst called the Pentagon and discussed the new order of battle with DIA analysts. After long talks and the forwarding of the analysis and raw data upon which the order of battle was based, the Washington analysts agreed that the new document was more correct than the existing one. With the launch of the ground offensive only two days away, it was an awkward time to change the basic intelligence picture for the theater. The DIA deferred to the theater director of intelligence, General Leide, the decision to issue a major change in the Iraqi order of battle. Leide called a meeting of his senior officers to discuss the pros and cons of reissuing the intelligence estimate just prior to the battle. I attended as the liaison to the C3IC.

Since only the names of the units were changed on the order of battle maps—and not the numbers of Iraqi tanks, artillery, or troops—the question arose as to whether it was worth the trouble and possible confusion to issue a major change in the order of battle itself. The majority of the officers did not want to change the maps, citing the confusion it would cause. They reasoned that if a coalition commander was about to engage an enemy force consisting of two infantry divisions assessed as "combat effective," it mattered little if they were named the 20th and the 48th Infantry Divisions. On the surface, these officers were probably right.

Others, including me, insisted that the issue went beyond that. For instance, we argued, what if our radio intercept units were able to report that the commander of the 20th Infantry Division had just ordered his units to don gas masks in preparation for a nerve gas artillery barrage against attacking coalition forces? If coalition commanders believed themselves to be facing the 20th Infantry Division, it follows that they would believe their units were about to be attacked with chemical weapons. More importantly, perhaps, no coalition commander facing the actual 20th Division would be aware of an impending chemical warfare event.

General Leide personally made the difficult and unpopular decision to reissue the order of battle; he chose to take the criticism rather than to allow a situation to exist where lives might have been jeopardized. It was simply the right thing to do. It was a lot of work, but when U.S. and coalition forces launched the attack, they knew exactly whom they were facing.

Several factors played into the decision to launch the ground offensive, not the least of which was pragmatism. There was concern among U.S.

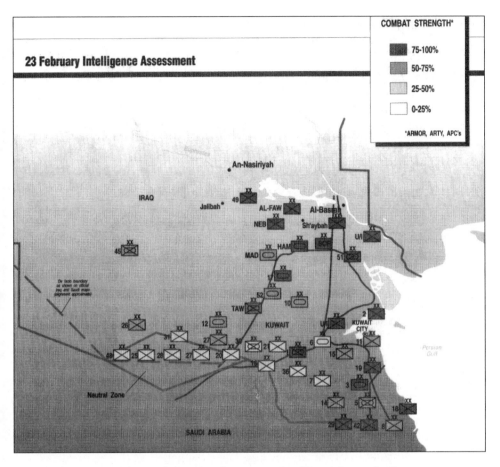

Deployment and remaining combat strength of Iraqi forces in the Kuwait Theater of Operations, 23 February 1991. *DOD*

Army and U.S. Marine officers that the overwhelming success of the air campaign might, for the first time in history, cause a war to be won— or at least the military objectives of a war to be achieved—without ground action by the victor. Some analysts were on the verge of declaring that Iraq would capitulate under another week of air bombardment. If the Iraqis were to state their intention to leave Kuwait prior to the initiation of the ground offensive, they might escape with much of their combat power intact, leaving Baghdad the wherewithal to continue its past pattern of unacceptable behavior. Politically, the coalition would not be able to mount a punishing ground campaign against a withdrawing Iraqi army.

On more than one occasion, senior army and marine officers at CENTCOM headquarters could be overheard stating that it was essential the ground campaign be launched immediately to ensure that the army and the marines had their opportunity to engage the Iraqis in combat. Only a successful ground operation could protect future budget allocations that might otherwise go toward air force and navy aircraft research, development, and acquisition.

The ground campaign kicked off in the early morning hours of 24 February. Two U.S. Marine divisions made the initial coordinated thrusts into the heart of Iraqi forces in central Kuwait. At the same time, the Saudi-Muslim Joint Forces Command–East attacked north up the Kuwaiti coast. Far to the west, the U.S. XVIII Airborne Corps with the French 6th Armored Division attached launched a run for the Euphrates River, combining fast-moving armor and a massive helicopter air assault deep into Iraqi territory. The main thrust, conducted by the heavy U.S. VII Corps with the U.S. 1st Infantry Division and British 7th Armoured Division attached, combined with a supporting assault by the Arab (Egyptian-Syrian) corps, was to kick off the next day.

Shortly after the initial attacks into Kuwait, intelligence sources inside Kuwait City reported that Iraqi soldiers had destroyed the desalinization plant that supplied the entire metropolitan area with potable water. To the analysts at CENTCOM, this could only mean that the Iraqis were planning to leave; an army that intended to remain would not disrupt its sole supply of fresh water. The destruction of the plant caused concern, however, that Iraqi forces might escape the impending trap as the heavy U.S., British, and French units moved northeast into southern Iraq and northern Kuwait.

Since the initial reports from the battlefields indicated progress far ahead of schedule, General Schwarzkopf directed his staff to consider the possibility of moving the start of the main attack forward by twelve hours and then placed a call to the Egyptian commander to ask him if he would be able to start that soon. It is accepted that when dealing in the Middle East, particularly with Arabs, you will not normally receive a negative answer to any request you make. True to form, when asked by General Schwarzkopf if he could launch his attack early, the Egyptian general immediately replied that he could.

One of the U.S. Army's foremost experts on the Middle East, Col. Jim Ritchey, was on duty in the command center during Schwarzkopf's conversation with the Egyptian commander. Considered the dean of military Arabists, Ritchey had served more tours in the region—including service as the U.S. defense and army attaché in Baghdad during the Iraqi invasion of Kuwait—than any other officer in the U.S. military. He advised the director of intelligence that although the Egyptian general said he could move twelve hours ahead of schedule, the Egyptian planning process was such that a schedule change of twelve hours was impossible.

The director of intelligence, Gen. Jack Leide, asked for a moment with Schwarzkopf and introduced Ritchey to the general. Ritchey, who had spent a considerable amount of time training with the Egyptian forces, explained to Schwarzkopf that neither the Egyptian planning system nor its command structure could accommodate a dramatic schedule change in such a short period of time. Schwarzkopf looked at Ritchey and, with a little indignation, reminded him that an Egyptian general officer had given his word on that question. Ritchey acknowledged that the Egyptian would likely answer in the affirmative but reiterated that his system could not accommodate the request. Schwarzkopf said he would take the word of a fellow general officer, dismissing both Leide and Ritchey.

As predicted, the Egyptians moved on the original schedule—that is, twelve hours after Schwarzkopf wanted them to go. When Egyptian forces reached their first objective ahead of the planned timeline, having encountered little resistance, they stopped and waited in order to remain strictly on schedule rather than press the attack. This pause allowed Iraqi artillery units to zero in on the halted Egyptian forces and kill and wound several soldiers.

Almost immediately after the initiation of hostilities, the threshold for the release of sensitive U.S. intelligence information was lowered, allowing a flow of tactical, actionable intelligence to reach frontline U.S. and coalition commanders. The release of certain data often revealed the method of collection or the ability of American intelligence to exploit a particular source of information. While it was not a problem for cleared U.S. commanders, the release of such information to foreign officers may have compromised sources and methods that we might need someday to use against these same countries or their allies and clients. Of particular sensitivity was information provided by the National Security Agency (NSA).

Once the ground war was launched, the flow of time-sensitive data from the NSA increased dramatically. We were authorized by General Schwarzkopf to release much of the information to the coalition after some minor "sanitization"—removal of a few handling instructions on the messages. Under intelligence community regulations, once U.S. troops are committed to combat, the cognizant authority for release of U.S. intelligence information shifts from the intelligence community to the theater combatant commander.

Only minutes after it was available to us, we were able to provide a wealth of information to U.S. and coalition commanders actively engaging Iraqi forces. Once the ground campaign was launched, the C3IC erupted into a frantic, short-fuzed command and control center that was passing information to the commanders who needed it as fast as it could be received and, if necessary, translated.

After the cessation of hostilities, we received a message from the NSA asking us to detail what we had done with each of the thousands of tactical reports provided to the C3IC in support of frontline commanders. Along with the listing of each report, they wanted to know who had released it, to whom it had been released, and who had seen it at the receiving unit. Anyone who had been in the C3IC during the frenzy of the ground campaign—papers literally flying everywhere—knew that answering this request was impossible.

By the time the decision was made to halt offensive operations against the Iraqis, coalition forces had liberated Kuwait with few losses, taken scores of thousands of Iraqis prisoner, and occupied hundreds of square miles of Iraqi territory. Despite the severity of the defeat, the Iraqi forces had apparently not used chemical or biological weapons—even though the majority of intelligence analysts in Riyadh and Washington had expected some use of chemical warfare agents, especially by Republican Guard units defending Iraqi soil. The question remains: why did the Iraqis not employ a proven weapon they knew thoroughly and had used successfully against the Iranians?

Iraq's intended or actual use of chemical weapons was one of the highest priority information requirements for the entire intelligence community. The question was asked of virtually every prisoner of war interrogated during the conflict (not all of them could be questioned after their numbers had climbed into the tens of thousands). From what we were able to piece together in Riyadh, chemical weapons had been brought from storage sites in southern Iraq, including the now-famous depot at Al-Khamisiyah, into Kuwait and placed into bunkers.[2] We knew for certain that Iraqi units had brought chemical decontamination equipment to southern Iraq and had set up decontamination sites in Kuwait, indicating at least their readiness to wage a chemical war.[3]

According to what we had determined Iraqi chemical warfare doctrine to be during the Iran-Iraq War, release authority for such weapons rested with the corps commanders. However, their using chemical weapons on ill-prepared Iranian forces who may or may not have been able to respond in kind was one thing. Using chemicals on well-trained and well-equipped American, British, and French troops, who would undoubtedly respond with superior, even nuclear, weapons, was another thing altogether. According to captured senior Iraqi officers, sometime in December, Saddam Husayn realized that the coalition was serious about a military confrontation over Kuwait—the United States was in the process of doubling its combat forces in the theater. He therefore ordered the chemical weapons to be returned to depots inside Iraq and withdrew the corps commanders' authority to release chemical weapons. Was Saddam convinced that use of chemicals on American, British, or French troops would provoke a chemical or even a nuclear response? According to his chief of military intelligence, Brigadier General Al-Samarra'i, he was.

Prior to the launch of the ground offensive, the U.S. State Department forwarded a diplomatic communication through international channels to its Iraqi counterpart. The message was very much to the point. Thus far in the war, the United States had bombed only military targets as well as Iraq's oil refineries and distribution network, leaving the oil fields themselves relatively untouched. However, if chemical weapons were used on American troops, the United States would destroy Iraq's ability to extract oil from the ground for years, possibly decades, to come. Along with a military defeat, Iraq would face economic devastation from which it would take a generation to recover. Although the message did not specifically articulate the threat of nuclear retaliation (nor was it ever seriously considered), that possibility was clearly implied.

At 8:00 P.M. on 1 March, the political leadership of the coalition made the decision to halt offensive operations. That decision—which was made in Washington, not Riyadh—was discussed in a series of conversations between General Powell at the Pentagon and General Schwarzkopf in Riyadh. Schwarzkopf had conferred with his subordinate commanders, who were concerned that they would not have enough time to destroy the Republican Guard divisions completely as they retreated toward Al-Basrah. Although the bridges over the Euphrates River had been destroyed by coalition aircraft strikes, Iraqi engineers had built several fords across shallow spots in the river, and a Republican Guard armored division was escaping to the north. Other Iraqi forces were heading toward the Iranian border east of Al-Basrah, crossing without stopping for border formalities and seeking refuge in Iran, much as the Iraqi Air Force had done weeks earlier.

American field commanders in southern Iraq had wanted another twenty-four hours to complete the job. To stop the escape of Republican Guard units to the north of the Euphrates, the XVIII Airborne Corps planned to conduct a massive helicopter air assault with the 101st Airborne Division, inserting them north of the river in the path of the escaping Iraqis. That maneuver was planned for 1 March, after the proposed cease-fire. With the 101st Division sitting north of the river to block the escape route, the Iraqis would be pressed by the combined VII and XVIII Corps, putting over seven heavy divisions on line moving east toward Al-Basrah. Stopping now would disrupt the plan to eliminate the Republican Guard's heavy divisions.

Political analysts at both the CIA and the DIA were concerned that, as the coalition ground offensive pushed further into Iraq and threatened the city of Al-Basrah, Iraq might collapse into three distinct enclaves—the Kurds in the north, the Sunni Muslims in the central region around Baghdad, and the Shi'a Muslims in the south. It had always been American policy that Iraq maintain its territorial integrity as one state, primarily to counterbalance future Iranian power in the region. The analysts were uncertain of Saddam Husayn's actions if faced with the disintegration of Iraq and resultant loss of power. According to Israeli analysts and former Iraqi DMI chief Wafiq Al-Samarra'i, Saddam may have opted to use his chemical and biological weapons as a last resort, despite the retaliation that would occur. Israeli analysts speculate that the firm possibility of Saddam's risking a biological-nuclear exchange with Israel was a key factor in President Bush's decision to end the war.[4]

The decision to suspend coalition offensive operations on 1 March has been, and will likely continue to be, the subject of extensive and intensive debate. In retrospect, many observers believe that we stopped too soon, that we should have destroyed more of the Iraqi forces on the move north of the Euphrates River that last day at Al-Basrah. Whether or not it was the right decision is now immaterial. One of the factors in the decision to stop the war four days after the beginning of the ground campaign was the mistaken idea that it could then be labeled a "hundred-hour war." Sounds good, but not quite accurate—it was a hundred-hour ground assault that was conducted in an area a hundred miles by two hundred miles and that concluded a forty-two-day war centered around a crippling, precision air campaign hitting targets in virtually every part of Iraq. The relative weight of air power versus ground maneuver will be hotly contested in the U.S. defense establishment for years to come. The Iraqi DMI, however, has acknowledged that Iraqi forces suffered the largest defeat in history, primarily as the result of the air campaign.[5]

While the decision to stop offensive operations was being considered in Washington, in Saudi Arabia there had already been a subtle shift in the attitudes of both the Arab and Muslim coalition military officers and the local Saudi population. In great measure this change had been brought about by the media's depiction of the gruesome nature of war as it was crystallized in the so-called highway of death. This now-famous stretch of highway led from the western edge of Kuwait City north through the Al-Jahra' pass and onto the four-lane desert highway to Iraq, the only major road out of the city to the north. The pass was a natural defense point and had been used as such by British forces in 1961 when Iraq threatened the newly independent state of Kuwait.

To defend the highway leading north to the Iraqi border, Iraqi combat engineers had sown extensive minefields on both sides of the road. Any attackers would be channeled to and through the narrow pass. These defenses were to create the conditions that led to the scene of destruction on the evening of 25 February. A U.S. Air Force F-15E fighter-bomber disabled an Iraqi vehicle in the pass, causing a major traffic backup that stretched for several miles. In the convoy were not only Iraqi tanks, armored personnel carriers, and military cargo trucks but also stolen Kuwaiti vehicles of every size and description, filled with loot taken from private homes, businesses, and public buildings.

Virtually everything of value was being carted back to Iraq in the continuing pillage of the oil-rich sheikhdom. When I walked through the wreckage and carnage on the road later that week, I was astounded by the variety of the items in the vehicles. Pianos, toilets, sinks, entire kitchens, light fixtures, furniture, tires, tools, medical supplies, clothing, foodstuffs, construction materials—everything. Even in retreat, Iraqi soldiers had given new meaning to the word "plunder."

With the pass ahead blocked and a continuous stream of American fighter aircraft bombing and strafing the convoy, many of the soldiers attempted to drive their vehicles into the desert rather than leave their loot—and in so doing, drove into the minefields laid by their own engineers. Those who did not get out of their vehicles on foot died on the road. Strictly speaking, the air attacks destroyed a convoy of tanks, armored personnel carriers, and military vehicles—all valid military targets. To many of our coalition allies, however, particularly the Arabs and Muslims, it was the United States, the superpower, killing defeated Arabs who were attempting to retreat from Kuwait.

The subtle distinction between military operations and the needless taking of Arab lives grew as pictures of the carnage on the road were shown repeatedly on news broadcasts around the world, including the Arab countries. In some of these countries, the popular impression of Desert Storm had changed from the liberation of Kuwait to the wanton killing of Arabs. Granted, one of the objectives of Desert Storm—one not often publicly acknowledged—was the destruction of Iraq's military machine. However, many of the Arab and Muslim coalition allies felt we were now crossing the line. To them, Kuwait had been liberated. It was time to stop the killing.

13

Safwan

With the fighting halted on 1 March, arrangements now had to be made to start a dialogue with the Iraqi leadership in Baghdad to impose a cease-fire and guarantee Iraq's adherence to the United Nations Security Council resolutions. Iraqi field commanders in the combat zone had to be contacted to ensure the fighting would remain halted. A misinterpretation on either side could easily ignite into a major battle, with needless loss of lives on both sides. American, British, and French forces now occupied about eighteen thousand square miles of Iraqi territory.

One problem in getting the message to the Iraqis was the virtual destruction of the communications system throughout their country. Through the good offices of the Soviet Foreign Ministry and its embassy in Baghdad as communications intermediaries, the Iraqis were told to meet the coalition commanders at an auxiliary airfield at Safwan, just north of the Kuwaiti border. For political reasons, Schwarzkopf decided that the location of the talks had to be inside Iraq. The initial meeting was scheduled for 2 March, but the destruction of all major bridges in Iraq by coalition air forces and the resulting chaos in the transportation system delayed the Iraqi generals' making the trip from Baghdad to Safwan until the next day. We were told by the Soviets that the Iraqis would be represented by Lt. Gen. Sultan Hashim Ahmad Al-Jabburi, the Iraqi armed forces deputy chief of staff for operations, and Lt. Gen. Salah 'Abbud Mahmud Al-Daghastani, commander of the now-destroyed III Corps. Both men were well known to U.S. intelligence through their distinguished combat records during the Iran-Iraq War. General Salah 'Abbud was the officer who had planned and executed the failed attack on Al-Khafji a month earlier. In his book *Desert Warrior,* General Khalid says that he could not get information from American forces on the two Iraqi generals and that he could not believe the U.S. intelligence services did not have biographies on these officers. As I recall, General Leide passed this information to his Saudi counterpart before the meeting at Safwan.

I was to be the lead interpreter at the meeting—an event that we were unsure how to label. General Schwarzkopf was adamant that he was not negotiating with the Iraqis, so use of the term "negotiations" was out. The Iraqis had not capitulated, so the use of the term "surrender" was inappropriate. In the end, we settled on "military-to-military talks." Obviously it was to be the most important interpreting task I had undertaken since my arrival in the theater seven months earlier, and it had to be done right. Two army colleagues assisted: Lt. Col. Steve Franke, a reserve officer fluent in the Saudi dialect, and CWO John Basilli, a native Arabic speaker serving with the U.S. VII Corps. Steve and I were to fly to Kuwait City and then on to Safwan, where John would be waiting.

We left Riyadh on a C-130 with several journalists, including Susan Spencer of CBS and Tom Brokaw of NBC. Neither of the journalists knew our final destination, only that we were being taken to Kuwait City and then on to the location of the talks. A CNN crew was also aboard with their satellite communications terminal, ready to begin broadcasting live as soon as we arrived at the "secret" location. Keeping geographic locations secret is difficult in the age of the Global Positioning System (GPS), accessible by anyone with a commercially available receiver. Minutes after arrival at the "undisclosed location," the CNN technicians had established a two-way satellite hookup to their headquarters in Atlanta, pulled out a GPS receiver, read off the coordinates, and asked, "Where are we?" In seconds, the response came back, "An airfield just outside Safwan, Iraq." So much for keeping the location secret.

The trip from Riyadh to Safwan had been sobering. All those going to Safwan met at Riyadh Air Base at 4:00 A.M. As we flew over the border at dawn from northern Saudi Arabia into Kuwait, we could see the oily black smoke from the hundreds of oil wells that made up the Al-Wafrah, Umm Qudayr, and Al-Burqan fields, set on fire by Iraqi forces to create obstacles for advancing coalition troops. As we arrived at what was left of the Kuwait International Airport, my attention was caught by the burned remains of a British Airways jet that had been trapped in Kuwait during the invasion—its passengers had become international pawns as Saddam's "guest" human shields. Inside the shell of what used to be a beautiful terminal building, virtually everything of value had been removed, even electrical switches and plumbing fixtures. What could not be removed had been destroyed.

As I stood on the runway waiting for the helicopters to take us to Safwan, all I could see in the early morning light were burning oil wells of the Al-Maqwah fields. Days earlier, this oil field had been the scene of a fierce battle during the capture of the airport by U.S. Marines in the face of stiff Iraqi resistance. I again assumed that the oil fires were ignited to create obstacles to impede the progress of the advancing coalition forces and to force them into minefields or zones susceptible to Iraqi artillery fire.

As the sun came up, we departed Kuwait International Airport heading north for Safwan on large U.S. Army CH-47 Chinook helicopters. As we got further north, I began to realize the reason the oil wells had been set ablaze, for the sprawling Al-Rawdatayn and Al-Rumaylah oil fields north of Kuwait City, which were the real treasures of the sheikhdom, were also on fire. These oil fields were not battlefields, so they had been set afire not as obstacles against advancing troops but out of spite and revenge. The image of hundreds of fires consuming millions of barrels of oil that are shooting hundreds of feet into the sky under fierce pressure is indescribable. If one can imagine hell, I think it would look like Kuwait's oil fields that day in March 1991. The helicopter bucked from the heat generated by the flames. Even today, when I look at the pictures I took from the helicopter, I cannot find the words to describe my awe at the magnitude of the destruction.

The mood on the helicopter was even more grim and somber than the flight from Riyadh to Kuwait City. The exhibition of the wanton destruction of Kuwait's airport, oil fields, and any other property of value was chilling. The material cost to the Iraqis was also evident. Hundreds of destroyed tanks and vehicles were scattered across the landscape. We passed over the Safwan border station, a familiar site from my past trips to Baghdad, now a charred skeleton of a once-vibrant commercial border city. Once we landed at Safwan Airfield, I looked south toward Kuwait. The fires and oily black smoke were easily visible from well inside Iraq. The trip had set the mood for the upcoming talks with the perpetrators of this destruction.

The U.S. 1st Infantry Division, the legendary "Big Red One," had secured Safwan Airfield. They had set up a homemade sign featuring their famous unit patch and the words "Welcome to Iraq—Courtesy of the Big Red One." The sign was a popular spot for souvenir photographs. All of the journalists and even the Saudi officers present for the talks had their photographs taken in front of the sign. An impressive show of American military power was on display. The entire area had been ringed with M-1 Abrams tanks and M-2 Bradley infantry fighting vehicles, while six fearsome-looking AH-64 Apache attack helicopters sat on the runway. In the center of the airfield was the U.S. flag on a high mast. It was a scene carefully orchestrated to send a strong message to the Iraqis coming to the talks.

The tent where the talks were to be held was set up at the northwest end of the runway at Safwan. Immediately adjacent was the administrative tent where security personnel would search all persons—Iraqi, American, and coalition—before allowing them to enter the meeting tent. It was in this tent that we surrendered all personal weapons. Anxious to prepare for the talks, I relinquished my pistol and went directly into the meeting tent, where I staked out the head of the table for myself by placing my notebooks and dictionaries there. The Iraqi officers would be to my right, and General Schwarzkopf and General Khalid to my left. My primary concern was that the two Iraqi generals would hear exactly what General Schwarzkopf was saying, through their interpreter. It was important that I check the interpretation provided by the Iraqi translator. General Khalid, who had been trained in the United Kingdom, had a superb command of the English language and did not need an interpreter.

Just after 11:30 A.M. I was called by one of General Schwarzkopf's aides and told to report immediately to the general. "Immediately" meant just that, so I quickly departed the tent without my hat and without retrieving my weapon. Stepping outside the tent, I saw General Schwarzkopf standing at the administrative tent awaiting the Iraqi delegation. He appeared impatient. I learned later that General Khalid had not yet arrived and Schwarzkopf was irritated. Rather than return to the meeting tent to get my hat, I walked up to the general and merely said, "Yes, sir."

He looked at me and said, "OK, Rick, here's how I want this to go. When the Iraqis arrive, I want you to go out there and find out who is in charge and have him get out of his vehicle. Then I want you to point to me and explain to him that I am unarmed. I will remove my weapons at that time. Escort him over here, and we will begin."

I asked Schwarzkopf how he wanted me to treat the Iraqi general—specifically, whether I should salute (awkward since I had left my hat in the tent). He told me not to salute but to be polite. As I walked out toward the northern edge of the circle of American tanks, I saw the Iraqi army UAZ-469, the Soviet equivalent of a Jeep, moving toward me, escorted by American "Humvees" (HMMWV—high mobility multipurpose wheeled vehicle) and an intimidating pair of Apache helicopters hovering barely above the ground. I waved to the Iraqi driver to stop, waited a few seconds for the helicopters to move away, and walked over to the passenger side of the Iraqi vehicle. There I saw an officer who matched the intelligence photograph of Lt. Gen. Sultan Hashim Ahmad Al-Jabburi. General Sultan Hashim looked the part of the stereotypical Iraqi tough guy—short, powerfully built, fair-skinned, dark hair, piercing eyes, the thick mustache favored by Saddam Husayn, and a scowl. I opened his door several inches and said in Arabic, "Good morning, sir. I am Major Francona from General Schwarzkopf's staff. If you will step out of the car, I will take you to meet the general, and we can begin."

At this moment, I was not aware of anything going on around me except the immediate task at hand. Unknown to me, the CNN crew that had flown up to Safwan from Riyadh was now broadcasting live via satellite, despite the fact that it was only 3:30 A.M. on the U.S. east coast. Attempting to follow my movements toward the Iraqis with their parabolic microphone, they had finally gotten the range correct and zeroed in on me. Fortunately, the next exchange with General Sultan Hashim was edited out of the later news broadcasts. I also saw no reason to bother General Schwarzkopf with an account of that particular conversation, although to this day my Arabic-speaking colleagues persist in reminding me of it.

After my polite introduction, the Iraqi general merely sat and glared at me. I was standing unarmed beside an Iraqi army jeep, two Iraqi generals within three feet, General Schwarzkopf was waiting for me to bring the Iraqis to him, and (although I did not realize it) the world was watching and listening on CNN. At this point, I was getting concerned and a

bit agitated. I had not used any Arabic words that could have been misunderstood or misconstrued—this was basic conversational stuff. I knew
the hard part would come later, during the actual talks. It had already
been a long day, it was far from over, and I already had a splitting
headache. I leaned closer and gruffly said the Arabic slang equivalent
of "Get out of the car, asshole." To my surprise (and relief), he smirked,
pushed open the door, and got out. As we walked to the administrative tent where General Schwarzkopf was standing, the Iraqi asked me,
"So, which one is Schwarzkopf?" I was somewhat surprised at the question. I assumed that anyone who was vaguely aware of recent events in
the Middle East would have recognized the imposing figure with four
stars on his hat.

General Schwarzkopf's first words were to me, not to General Sultan
Hashim. He told me to translate his words exactly to the Iraqi. He began,
"We will enter this tent, and everyone will be searched before we go into
the meeting place." I translated the words into Arabic; the Iraqi interpreter, a brigadier who had spent several years living in Michigan, nodded to Sultan Hashim that my translation was correct. This is a normal
action for an interpreter, ensuring that his principal was being properly served, and I took no offense. I planned to do the exact same thing
during the talks a few minutes later. General Sultan Hashim appeared
insulted at the mention of a search and became indignant. He said that
they were unarmed, having left their weapons in their vehicles. When
I relayed Sultan Hashim's protestations, General Schwarzkopf said that
everyone—no exception, no debate—who would enter the meeting
tent would be searched, in the interest of everyone's safety. The Iraqi
replied that he would consent only to a search by the senior American
officer, meaning Schwarzkopf.

General Schwarzkopf responded by ordering the U.S. security personnel to search him first. The security search was performed with an
electronic wand, similar to those used in commercial airports. When
General Sultan Hashim saw how General Schwarzkopf was being
searched, he moved forward and raised his arms. I think that he was
put at ease by the fact that the search was not a "hands on" pat down.
After a check of the others in the party, we all moved in a group to the
meeting tent.

Unfortunately, for the first few minutes after we had entered, the
tent took on a circus atmosphere. Since no reporters were to be present

during the actual talks, it was decided to allow a photo opportunity to the press pool. Generals Schwarzkopf and Khalid, representing the coalition forces, were to my left. The three Iraqi officers sat to my right, backs to the tent wall. As the Iraqis had brought no additional staff, the chairs along the tent wall that had been intended for the rest of the Iraqi delegation were empty. Since the remaining coalition commanders and representatives, totaling about fifty officers, were seated behind Schwarzkopf and Khalid facing the three Iraqis, it almost appeared that the Iraqis were on stage. With a dozen photographers flashing scores of pictures while the Iraqis sat stone-faced, it was humiliating for the three Iraqi officers. Had I not flown over the sacked and burning country of Kuwait a few hours earlier, I might have felt a twinge of compassion. A glance toward the south and the easily visible flames and smoke towering over the Kuwaiti oil fields renewed my revulsion at the senseless destruction—ravage that had been planned and executed by the Iraqi leadership whom these officers, two feet to my right, represented.

There was one brief spot of comedic relief in the grim setting. General Schwarzkopf preferred to drink Diet Pepsi, and his aides usually had a can of it already in position wherever he was going to sit. The Safwan meeting was no exception. As the photographers snapped their pictures, I looked at the table in front of me. There, amid drab brown notebooks and plastic water bottles, was a bright white and blue can of Diet Pepsi sitting in front of America's currently most recognizable hero. I remember thinking, *You can't buy this kind of advertising*—it was undoubtedly going to be the day's lead story of almost every print and broadcast news report on the planet.

After the media representatives left the tent, General Schwarzkopf began the meeting by explaining that the talks would now officially begin, all proceedings would be taped, and each side would be provided a copy of the tapes. General Sultan Hashim nodded silently, with apparent disdain. Those in attendance were struck by the obvious arrogance of the senior Iraqi officer, especially after the military defeat his forces had just endured.

The initial topic was prisoners of war. Schwarzkopf asked that there be an accounting of prisoners on both sides, that the International Committee of the Red Cross be provided with the information, and that the process of repatriation be arranged through that body. Agreeing immediately, Sultan Hashim unexpectedly took a folded piece of

paper from his pocket and read that Iraq was holding forty-one coalition prisoners and a small number of bodies, which he identified by
individual nationality. He apologized for not having the names. He also
said there were several unidentified bodies from a U.S. Air Force AC-130
gunship that had been shot down over Kuwait.

Sultan Hashim asked for a similar accounting of prisoners of war
from the coalition side. Schwarzkopf turned to one of his aides, who
handed him a thick computer printout. He told the Iraqi general that
as of the previous evening, the coalition had counted over sixty thousand Iraqi soldiers as prisoners of war but that the counting was still in
progress, so the total number would eventually be much greater. After
this number had been translated for Sultan Hashim, he appeared
stunned and became visibly less arrogant. He turned to General Salah
'Abbud, seated to his right, and asked if those numbers were accurate.
Salah 'Abbud, as the commander of III Corps, should have had an idea
of the number of Iraqis that had been captured. Instead, he quietly said
that he did not know but that it was possible. It was obvious that the full
extent of the Iraqi defeat in Kuwait and southern Iraq was not yet
known in Baghdad, a fact due to the coalition's almost complete destruction of Iraqi communications.

General Schwarzkopf then advised the Iraqis that coalition forces
had also captured several Yemeni and Sudanese volunteers serving with
Iraqi forces. General Sultan Hashim waved his hand and said that all of
his soldiers were Iraqis and that he knew nothing of any Yemenis or
Sudanese serving in his ranks. He suggested they be turned over to the
Red Cross. This was interesting, since the Yemeni and Sudanese governments had been very vocal in their support of Saddam Husayn and
his occupation of Kuwait. Both governments also claimed that "thousands" of their citizens had gone to Iraq to fight.

General Khalid asked about Kuwaitis being held in Iraq. General
Schwarzkopf indicated that these must also be included in the prisoner
of war accounting through the Red Cross. Sultan Hashim said that all
prisoners of war would be released. Khalid was concerned specifically
about Kuwaiti civilians who had been taken to Iraq. When translating
this exchange, we American interpreters noted that the Iraqis, both Sultan Hashim and his interpreter, used the Arabic word for "guests" rather
than the more correct "detainees" when referring to these Kuwaiti civilians. (The Arabic word for "prisoner of war" is very specific and only

applies to military prisoners, hence the use of a different term for the Kuwaiti civilians.)

I asked the interpreter to use our preferred term since we believed the word "guests" to be inappropriate. Indeed, the issue of Kuwait detainees in Iraq has never been resolved to the satisfaction of the Kuwaiti government. When we got a chance to speak to Husayn Kamil Al-Majid (son-in-law of Saddam Husayn and former Iraqi minister of defense) after his defection to Jordan in 1995, he was asked about the Kuwaiti detainees. With no visible remorse or emotion, he replied matter-of-factly that he thought they had all been killed.

The next topic raised to the Iraqi generals at the Safwan meeting was the establishment of a temporary demilitarized zone. General Schwarzkopf proposed that he and Sultan Hashim agree on a line from which both sides in the conflict would move back, simply as a means of putting some space between the armed combatants. Schwarzkopf explained to the Iraqi general that it was a good idea to separate the enemies—"young men with weapons"—from each other in order to prevent the kind of bloodshed that arises from misunderstandings, as had happened just a day earlier. Sultan Hashim said that this was Iraq and coalition forces should not be in Iraq since Iraqi forces had left Kuwait and that he could not, therefore, agree to demarcation lines. Schwarzkopf explained that this was not a political boundary or a new border but merely a no-contact line agreed to by military commanders to prevent further hostilities and casualties. Sultan Hashim agreed on the condition that in no way was this to be construed as a new border or a political cease-fire line inside sovereign Iraqi territory.

Schwarzkopf offered a map on which was drawn a proposed no-contact line. The Iraqi general asked why the line was drawn behind the forward line of Iraqi troops. Schwarzkopf said that this line was actually just short of where the coalition had stopped on the morning of 1 March and that it reflected the current position of American troops. Again looking stunned, Sultan Hashim turned to the III Corps commander. Salah 'Abbud replied that he did not know the exact position of the front lines but that the situation as indicated on the map was possible. We were struck by the fact that two full days after hostilities had halted, the Iraqi senior military leadership did not know how many men they had lost or how much Iraqi territory coalition forces had occupied. By now, Sultan Hashim appeared to have lost his arrogant facade and seemed fully resigned to accept the magnitude of Iraq's military defeat.

Schwarzkopf then told the Iraqi officers there were to be no more missile attacks on either Saudi Arabia or Israel. They agreed. Assuming it was his turn to make a request, Sultan Hashim asked if the U.S. Air Force would stop flying its jet fighters over Baghdad at all hours of the day and night. Schwarzkopf refused, saying that as long as Iraqi forces possessed the potential to threaten coalition forces, coalition aircraft would control Iraqi airspace.

At this point, Sultan Hashim raised an issue that still remains controversial and unresolved. Stating that coalition air strikes had destroyed many roads and bridges, he asked that Iraq be allowed to fly helicopters for the purpose of transporting officials from place to place. Schwarzkopf agreed that coalition forces would not fire on helicopters that did not pose a threat to those forces. As is now well known, the Iraqis fully exploited this apparent loophole by using their helicopter gunships to brutally crush the Shi'a rebellion that began in the southern part of the country immediately after the end of the war with the coalition. Whether or not this request was a calculated ploy by the Iraqis is uncertain to this day.

Schwarzkopf then asked the Iraqis to provide maps of all minefields they had laid on land and deployed in the waters off Kuwait and in the Persian Gulf itself. The Iraqis said they would provide map overlays with the location of minefields at follow-on meetings. One of the problems with the Iraqi map overlays, however, was the difference in map scales. The U.S. and coalition forces used 1:250,000 or 1:50,000 scale maps. Iraqi military maps were 1:100,000. When the minefield maps were delivered, we found them to be hand-drawn tracing-paper overlays with only rough coordinates. Although we were able to convert the Iraqi overlays to match the scale of our maps, the inaccuracy of the original overlays was so great that they were useless except to indicate that a minefield existed in a certain area. Therefore, rather than being able to go to the precise location of a mine, we would have to sweep each designated area completely. This was a far cry from the stringent location reporting requirements for U.S. mine emplacements.

After the establishment of procedures for periodic follow-up coordination meetings between Iraqi and American officers at a nearby road junction, the meeting ended. The Iraqis were much more at ease and decidedly less arrogant than when they had arrived. After exchanging salutes and handshakes with Schwarzkopf and Khalid, they quickly left the area. The two coalition generals held a press conference outside the tent.

It all ended very abruptly. My work was done. I hopped a ride back to Kuwait on a Saudi army helicopter and then back to Riyadh on an air force transport. Somehow it didn't seem as though we had come to any true closure. The fighting was over. The conflict was not.

14

Safwan Two

On 15 March, the Iraqis sent a letter to General Schwarzkopf via the liaison contact point at Safwan, following communications procedures that had been established at the coalition-Iraqi military-to-military talks two weeks earlier. A preliminary translation was faxed to CENTCOM headquarters from the VII Corps liaison office at Safwan. In the letter, the Iraqis notified the coalition that on 18 March they would begin moving their fighter aircraft from secondary and dispersal airfields back to their principal air bases. These aircraft had been dispersed during the coalition air strikes after it had become apparent that the previously secret "black program" American weapons could penetrate Iraq's Yugoslav-built HASs (hardened aircraft shelters).

The letter stated that the aircraft needed to be returned for maintenance and included a detailed schedule of the proposed movements so that the coalition would not shoot down the Iraqi fighters during these short transit flights. The letter did not mention the aircraft that remained parked at or near such archeological treasures as the Babylonian ziggurats, the ancient pyramidal structures near An-Nasiriyah. The Iraqis had been correct in their assessment that coalition planners would not strike aircraft near these cultural sites for fear of damaging important pieces of history.

When it arrived at CENTCOM headquarters in Riyadh, the letter caused an immediate reaction. It did not request a waiver to the agreed-upon prohibition against Iraqi fixed-wing flight activity; rather, it declared an intention to conduct the movements. This attitude, some-times labeled "Baghdad arrogance," is fairly typical. If not challenged, the Iraqis would have achieved their goal, winning a de facto change in agreements made at Safwan. The liaison officer at Safwan also faxed the original Arabic text in case we wanted to check their translation. I read over the text myself. Having only a few minor word changes that were a matter of personal preference rather than anything that changed the meaning, the translation accurately conveyed the declarative nature of the original letter. The Iraqis were stating what they intended to do; their letter made no requests and asked no questions.

General Schwarzkopf was emphatic in his reaction. As long as Amer-ican forces were in southern Iraq, there would be no Iraqi fixed-wing flight activity anywhere in Iraq, period. He regarded the situation with such gravity that he instructed his chief of staff, General Johnston, to meet personally with the Iraqis at Safwan and explain to them that the coalition—especially the United States, whose troops comprised the bulk of coalition forces—was serious about the flight ban. Any violations of that ban, including the intended short flights described in the letter, would result in the planes' being shot down. The Iraqi aircraft were to remain where they were.

On 17 March, General Johnston, two members of his staff, and I flew aboard General Schwarzkopf's C-21 jet to Kuwait City and then on to Safwan on a U.S. Army Blackhawk helicopter. Again we flew over the burning oil fields of Kuwait, still spewing millions of barrels of flaming oil into the air every day and sending thick black clouds of smoke hun-dreds of miles long across the Middle East and south Asia. Again we flew over the "highway of death," a still-visible reminder of the avarice of the Iraqi occupation forces and the devastating effect of American air power. We landed at the intersection of the Safwan and Az-Zubayr highways on what had once been a busy cloverleaf that I had used many times in 1988 on my drives between Baghdad and Kuwait. Now it was an American mil-itary camp ringed with M-1 tanks. A tent that had been set up was flying an American flag and an orange flag, indicating that the Iraqi officers could approach this point to talk to the coalition forces occupying the southern portion of their country.

When the Saudis heard that General Johnston was going to meet with senior Iraqi officers at Safwan, they said they would like to send a senior officer to speak to the Iraqis about prisoner of war repatriation operations. By this time, all coalition prisoners that the Iraqis claimed to have captured had been returned. The Saudis wanted to increase the speed with which the tens of thousands of Iraqi prisoners of war were being returned to Iraqi control. They also wanted to demand an accounting of remaining coalition prisoners held by Iraq—a group that, according to the Kuwaitis and the Saudis, consisted of hundreds, possibly thousands, of Kuwaitis who had been forcibly detained in Iraq since the invasion in August.

Shortly after our arrival at Safwan, Maj. Gen. Yusif Madani, the Joint Forces Command director of operations, arrived in a Saudi helicopter and joined General Johnston's party. I suspect that General Madani had been sent by General Khalid to ensure that senior U.S. officers did not meet with the Iraqis without a senior Saudi officer present to maintain the appearance of a coalition effort. Sharing in the translation tasks that day was U.S. Army major (now colonel) Bernie Dunn. Bernie, the senior VII Corps interpreter, was an experienced Middle East specialist who had fought the war as an advisor and liaison officer to the commander of the Egyptian corps. He and I had already discussed how we would handle the interpretation tasks. We both hoped it would be a quick meeting because the midday heat could become oppressive, especially in the confines of the tent. As Bernie and I were setting up our materials, the Iraqis arrived amid a cloud of dust and the roar of the two Bradleys that were escorting their Soviet UAZ field sedan.

The two Iraqi generals strode into the tent and glared at us with the arrogance that was characteristic of senior Iraqi officers forced to deal with the Americans. I looked at Bernie with a "who are these guys?" expression on my face. Bernie whispered that the senior officer, a major general, was the area commander and appeared at Safwan only if a serious matter was to be discussed. Normally, the general had to be summoned from Al-Basrah, and it was clear he did not enjoy being in an area of Iraq that was under the control of American forces. The other general, a brigadier, was unknown to us, but he looked more like an accountant than a combatant. As Bernie went over to show the Iraqis to their places, their interpreter, a major, walked in.

I was stunned to be now face-to-face with Majid Al-Hilawi, whom I had not seen since my last night in Baghdad at the end of the U.S.-Iraqi military relationship in 1988. Not quite sure how to comport ourselves in this awkward situation, we both merely turned and took our seats and looked at each other. My old friend appeared to be much thinner and a lot older, and his thick hair seemed grayer than three years should have caused. There was no time now for us to have a lengthy discussion, so while Bernie attended to getting the Iraqi generals settled, I simply walked over to where Majid was sitting and offered my hand, which he took warmly. He stood, smiled, and said in his thick Iraqi accent, "I wondered when we would meet again." I asked about his wife and children. He said that he had gotten them to his parents' home in Babylon before the air war had started and that they were as well as could be expected, given the situation and the effect of the sanctions. The chief of the Iraqi delegation, a major general, observed us talking amiably and asked me if I knew the major. I said that I had known him "a long time ago, in Baghdad—when things were different." He nodded and indicated that he was ready to begin. Majid's smile disappeared, and we became what we were at that moment in time—officers of opposing forces. I departed the tent to escort General Johnston to the meeting.

The discussions were heated, as we had expected them to be, and Majid and I each adopted the hostile persona of our respective leadership. The Iraqis began to plead their case for moving the aircraft back to their parent bases, claiming that these short flights were for maintenance and posed no threat to coalition forces. General Johnston cut them off and firmly reiterated General Schwarzkopf's guidance that no Iraqi fixed-wing flights were permitted while U.S. forces remained in Iraq and appropriate United Nations controls were not yet in place. Johnston went on to explain that he had come to Safwan personally at General Schwarzkopf's direction to explain the seriousness with which the coalition viewed the prohibition on Iraqi fixed-wing flight activity. He went on to indicate U.S. displeasure with Iraqi use of helicopter gunships against the Shi'a rebellion in the south and the Kurds in the north. Johnston reminded the Iraqis that the coalition had agreed to Iraqi helicopter flights for logistics reasons because of the extensive damage to Iraqi roads and bridges. The sanction was never meant as a license for Iraqi aerial bombardment of its own population.

At this point, the second Iraqi general, who until now had been silent, spoke up. It became apparent to Bernie and me that this officer, the one I had thought looked like an accountant, was from Baghdad, most likely from the Directorate of Military Intelligence. He countered Johnston's remarks about the armed helicopter activity by claiming that the Shi'a rebellion was actually an operation sponsored and instigated by Iranians inside Iraq and that the combatants were actually Iranian Islamic Revolutionary Guard Corps (IRGC) officers. The Iraqi general offered to provide identification cards from IRGC officers captured inside Iraq as proof that the Iranians were responsible. He claimed that Iran was taking advantage of Iraq's problems with the United States to reignite the "First Gulf War" and that Iraq was entitled to defend itself. As I translated this particular statement for General Johnston, I cast a disbelieving glance toward Majid. He looked down and away as if he knew this was merely the "party line" and not the whole truth.

Although it was in fact the party line, there was some element of truth to the Iraqi claims. Soon after the cessation of coalition offensive operations, small numbers of the Iranian-sponsored Al-Badr Corps had infiltrated into the Al-Basrah area and begun fomenting the Shi'a uprising. The Al-Badr Corps was composed of Iraqi Shi'a guerrillas who had gone to Iran for training and support. The organization responsible for training and equipping the Al-Badr Corps was (and remains) the IRGC. It is conceivable, even likely, that some of those IRGC officers had accompanied the Al-Badr Corps into southern Iraq. The Iranians used the Al-Badr Corps as a surrogate force much as the Iraqis used the Mujahidin-e Khalq, an Iranian guerrilla group based in, and supported by, Iraq.

I scribbled a note to that effect for General Johnston on my pad so he knew not only the words being said but my impression of the tone and inflection behind them. Johnston deflected the Iraqi justification of the use of armed helicopters, stating that the United States and the coalition remained concerned over the helicopters and that should the choppers be perceived as posing any threat to U.S. or coalition forces, they would be shot down.

Once the Iraqi generals realized that the topic of transferring their aircraft was not negotiable and General Johnston did not wish to discuss further the alleged Iranian incursion, they turned to General Madani to discuss Iraqi prisoner of war repatriation from Saudi Arabia. The discussions now were between the Iraqi and Saudi generals, entirely in Arabic. Up until now, everything had been done by sequential translation. The Iraqi general would speak, then pause. I would take notes and, at the pause, translate what had been said into English for General Johnston. General Johnston would answer and then pause. At the pause,

Majid would translate what had been said into Arabic for the Iraqi general. Sequential translation is sometimes preferred because it gives the principals more time to think between exchanges, and it gives the interpreters a chance to monitor each other's translations for accuracy. However, since the principals in the Iraqi-Saudi conversation were both Arabic speakers, I had to do a simultaneous translation for General Johnston.

While the Saudi and Iraqi generals discussed logistics arrangements for the repatriation of Iraqi prisoners of war, I sat to Johnston's side, slightly behind him, and in a low voice translated both sides of the Arabic conversation as it happened. The thrust of the conversation was a Saudi desire to return as many as five thousand Iraqi prisoners per day and an Iraqi reluctance to accept any more than fifteen hundred, based on the logistics and transportation problems on the Iraqi side. The Saudis wanted to get the Iraqis out of Saudi Arabia as fast as possible. The Iraqis, on the other hand, were busy using their remaining logistics capabilities to support counterinsurgency operations in the south against the Shi'a uprising and in the north against a Kurdish uprising. Handling returning prisoners of war was not their number-one priority. In the end, the Saudis realized there was no way to force a higher number on the Iraqis.

After the discussions about prisoner repatriation were concluded, all the general officers stood, shook hands without smiling, and departed. The Americans and Saudis left the tent together and then went their separate ways. General Johnston headed for the VII Corps liaison tent to place a secure call to advise General Schwarzkopf that the Iraqis clearly understood that any fixed-wing aircraft would be shot down if they took off.

I took advantage of the time to speak with Majid. As the Iraqi generals waited for their vehicle to be permitted back into the cantonment area, Majid and I reminisced about the times we had spent together in Baghdad in 1988, and we shook our heads wondering how it had come to this. We talked about how we both had fully expected to meet again during the war, since we shared similar backgrounds, but we had not thought we would be facing one another as the enemies we now indeed were. I asked how he had been, remarking that he appeared to have lost some weight. He glanced at the ground and said quietly that it had been "a difficult time." I took this to mean that food shortages were still a problem. I asked one of the American sergeants if they had some MREs (meals ready to eat) to spare. He said they had more than they wanted—MREs were not generally regarded as favorites by U.S. servicemembers—so I asked if he could discreetly throw a couple of cases of the rations into the Iraqi vehicle. He just looked at me. I explained that the Iraqi major standing next to me was an old friend—I think I told him we had gone to college together in Michigan or some-such nonsense. He shrugged and said, "Why not? The war's over, right?"

Majid quietly tried to thank me. I could tell he was embarrassed, so I changed the subject and asked about acquaintances we had both known in Baghdad and Washington. I asked him to extend my best wishes to Brig. Gen. Wafiq Al-Samarra'i, now the director of Iraqi military intelligence, who had been the officer I had worked closely with in Baghdad during the 1988 U.S.-Iraqi military cooperation. For some reason, it did not strike me as strange that I was passing personal regards to the chief of the enemy's military intelligence service. While I realized the Iraqi armed forces were the enemy, I had never personalized the conflict—a difficult position to maintain, given the unnecessary and wanton destruction of Kuwait at the Iraqis' hands. I did not ask about Gen. Nabil Sa'id, the former military attaché to Washington, because I knew he had been executed for no other reason than his being regarded as having gotten too close to the Americans.

For all the time Majid and I had spent together, and the camaraderie between us that had been built on the experiences we shared three years ago, our relationship was in the past. We were friendly toward each other now, but it would never be the same again. Too much had happened in the interim, and it appeared that our countries would remain enemies for the foreseeable future. It was time for him to go. I gripped his hand tightly, putting my left hand on his right shoulder—this was as close to an embrace we felt comfortable with, given the uniforms we wore and the place we were in. He returned the handshake, gave me a light punch with his left hand, nodded his head, and walked away. He did not look back, nor did I expect him to. I watched as the Iraqi UAZ sedan moved into a column with the American tracked vehicles and sped away in a cloud of dust. I have not seen or heard from him since.

After the talks were completed at Safwan, General Johnston and I boarded the helicopter for the return flight to Kuwait. Our flight from Kuwait City back to Riyadh was not scheduled for another few hours, although the plane was at General Johnston's disposal. Having completed our objectives early and with good results, General Johnston decided to take advantage of the extra time to observe from the air the battle damage to Kuwait. He asked the helicopter pilot to take us on a tour of the area on the way back to Kuwait International Airport.

We headed down the main highway from Safwan, taking detours to observe damage inflicted by both sides. Again, we flew near the burning oil wells. It is hard to comprehend the destruction and even harder to understand the reasoning behind the order to ignite the wells and risk ecological damage whose repercussions could not be imagined. To give us a close-up view, the pilot maneuvered the helicopter close to an oil well sending forth flaming oil in gushes that, under tremendous pressure, spewed hundreds of feet into the air. The roar of the fire was easily heard over the noise of the helicopter engines and rotors. As we neared the column of flames, the helicopter windows grew hot to the touch, and the helicopter started to buck from the heat waves given off by the fire. I photographed several of the wells and the fields on fire, a collection of pictures that I have titled "Saddam's Inferno." Though initial studies indicated that some of the wells might never be fully extinguished, American technological skill proved that prediction wrong.

After leaving the oil fields, we flew over the highway of death again. Even after two weeks, charred bodies remained in the burned-out vehicles. It would take several more weeks to remove all of these bodies and clear the debris from the roadway. From there, we flew over 'Ali Al-Salim Air Base. This was a Kuwaiti air base that had been taken over by the Iraqis shortly after the invasion. Although the Iraqis never moved fighter or other combat aircraft forward to use this base, they did use the hardened aircraft shelters (HAS) to store weapons and high-value military equipment.

During Desert Shield and Desert Storm, we had reports from Iraqi deserters and the Kuwaiti resistance that the Iraqis were storing Scud missile TEL (transporter erector launcher) vehicles in the shelters. We suspected that what the sources had seen were actually the smaller FROG (free-rocket-over-ground) battlefield support rocket TELs. Either way, both the FROG rockets and the Scud missiles were capable of carrying chemical warheads and were a threat to coalition forces. The HASs on 'Ali Al-Salim were targeted for strikes with penetrating laser-guided bombs. When struck with the penetrating weapons, the HAS would normally contain the subsequent explosion, compressing any-thing inside the shelter into its reinforced walls. As a result, it would have a hole in its top, and the debris that had been forced out of its doors and vents would be visible. However, one HAS was completely obliterated. Whatever had been stored in that HAS was extremely explosive, and though no one really knows for sure what it was, it is believed to have been some sort of liquid-fueled rocket or missile. After tours of a few more battle-damaged areas, we returned to Kuwait International Airport, which was still undergoing cleanup, and flew to Riyadh.

15

Aftermath

One of the problems with the commitment of troops to a military campaign is the process of disengaging. Once U.S. forces have been deployed to a theater of operations, it often becomes difficult to gauge when their mission is complete and they can be withdrawn without negating the results of their actions.

In the case of Kuwait, the stated goals of the deployment of American forces for both Desert Shield and Desert Storm were quite clear. The objective of the former was the defense of Saudi Arabia against Iraqi attack—something that became a distinct possibility after Iraq's invasion of Kuwait. The objective of the latter was the liberation of Kuwait—a goal that would be accomplished by ejecting Iraqi forces from that country. And there were other, not publicly stated, U.S. objectives for Desert Storm: the destruction of Iraqi chemical, biological, and nuclear weapons programs and the ballistic missile systems designed to carry them; and the eradication of the Iraqi armed forces' ability to mount a credible threat to its Arab and Israeli neighbors. However, the effort to destroy Iraq's war machine was not to go so far as to cause either of two possible undesired outcomes. First, caution had to be taken to ensure that Iraq was not so weak that it might become an irresistible target for Iranian opportunism—Tehran was still smarting from its military defeat by the Iraqis less than three years earlier. Secondly, Iraq had to remain intact as a single country. A central government too weakened by the coalition might not be able to defend itself successfully against either Shi'a or Kurdish forces intent on creating autonomous entities.

The goals of the U.S. military operations had been largely met by 1 March, when the coalition ceased offensive operations in the KTO. The goals were within reach when the Iraqis accepted United Nations Security Council resolutions calling for supervised destruction of advanced weapons and continuous monitoring of its weapons-capable facilities and industries. Monitoring and enforcement of the resolutions was now a UN responsibility, although much of the expertise, technology, and information gathering to support the effort would be provided by the United States.

After the meetings at Safwan, there was still much to be done in the theater. While Iraq turned its attention toward the Shi'a insurgency in the south and the Kurdish uprising in the north, the coalition began a survey of the area under its control. Included in the thousands of square miles of Iraqi territory were a major air base, some smaller dispersal airfields, a regional air defense–sector operations center, numerous military storage areas and bunkers, and several towns and cities. The orders from Riyadh were to destroy all equipment that still had military utility. Certain items, of course, had value for the U.S. intelligence community, yet army units were sometimes destroying equipment so fast that intelligence officers learned of its existence only after its destruction. For example, after elements of the 24th Mechanized Infantry Division captured Tallil Air Base, they reported to their parent headquarters that there was a "small aircraft" in one of the hangars and that they were going to destroy it unless told otherwise. When the air force intelligence officers in Riyadh saw the words "small aircraft," they assumed it was a light plane, such as an observation craft. When the air force exploitation team came to inspect the nearby air defense–sector operations center, they were disheartened to find that what the soldiers had destroyed was an almost new, late-version MiG-29 Fulcrum, the Soviets' top fighter aircraft.

Back in Riyadh, the Saudis watched and waited to see if the Americans would honor their word to depart the kingdom once the mission had been accomplished. Most of the American troops in the kingdom had had their fill of the harsh environment, the difficulty in working with the Saudis, and the restrictions on most forms of recreation imposed to appease their hosts. They were ready to go home.

In the Saudi command post, more than one Saudi officer asked when the Americans would be leaving the kingdom. Many Saudis felt they had been forced to make too many concessions to those of us who were now present in their country, and they were eager to get back to what they viewed as normal day-to-day life. In April 1991, most of the American combat troops began to withdraw from the battlefields of Iraq and Kuwait back to Saudi Arabia and, from there, returned to their home garrisons in the United States or Germany.

16

Title V

I returned home in late March with the bulk of the CENTCOM staff aboard a chartered Pan American Airways 747. We were tired of Saudi Arabia, and many of us were tired of the Saudis themselves. We all enjoyed a laugh when the pilot informed us that we had left Saudi airspace with his announcement that we could now set our watches ahead six hundred years. It was a crowded, long flight (although no one complained)—seven hours to Rome, where we faced a lengthy delay because of an airport strike. But once the Italian airport authorities learned that the aircraft was a returning Desert Storm charter, the striking unions went back to work long enough to get us off the ground.

From Rome, we flew ten hours nonstop to New York's JFK Airport for a refueling stop. As we were roaming around the airport, people cheered and greeted us—a reception quite a bit different from what I had encountered on my return from Vietnam eighteen years earlier. When we found an open bar (we had not been able to drink during our entire time in Saudi Arabia), we could not buy our own drinks. Passers-by would not let us take out our wallets, and the waitresses would not accept our tips. It was good to be back in the United States!

Some of us were surprised by the overwhelmingly favorable public reaction to several hundred American troops wandering around JFK in desert-camouflage battle dress. Most of us had been gone since August or September and were unaware of the level of public support for the troops deployed to the Persian Gulf. Our primary, and often sole, source

of civilian news was CNN and occasional ABC, CBS, or NBC news broadcasts carried on AFRTS. My impression had been that protests against
our actions in the Gulf were widespread. That impression was corrected
only after I had returned home and spoken to many of my neighbors.

Finally, when we took off for MacDill Air Force Base, many of us were
sleepy from the first beer we'd had in many months. After a relatively
short flight, we were greeted in Florida by a military band and a large
crowd. As I walked out of the aircraft and down the steps, I was met by
air force colonel Karl Polifka (CENTCOM's deputy director of intelligence) and his wife, Lois, who was holding a six-pack with my name
on it. I knew I was on my way home.

From here, the situation continued to get even better. A general officer from the DIA was there, calling out the names of all those persons
from Washington-area units who had been attached to CENTCOM. He
had arranged an Air Force Reserve C-130 to fly us immediately to Andrews
Air Force Base, Maryland—home. The DIA had contacted all of our
families so they could meet the plane. It was well past midnight when
the transport landed at Andrews. In addition to our families, hundreds
of "greeters" were there—anonymous volunteers who came to make
sure everyone returning from the Gulf would be welcomed home at
any hour of the day or night.

I returned to work to find that I had been reassigned to the Office
of the Secretary of Defense (OSD)—specifically, to the assistant secretary tasked to write the report to Congress on the conduct of the war.
Congress mandated the "Report to Congress on the Conduct of the
Persian Gulf War, Pursuant to Title V of the Persian Gulf War Supple-
mental Authorization and Personnel Benefits Act of 1991" when it provided the funds for operations Desert Shield and Desert Storm. Commonly called the "Title V Report," it was to be drafted by the assistant
secretary of defense for strategy and resources and sent to Congress
over the signature of the secretary of defense. A senior staff member
from that office, army colonel George Raach, was placed in charge of
the effort and told to form a team from the services and agencies
involved. I was assigned to represent the intelligence community. Other
members of the team represented the U.S. Air Force, Army, Navy, Marine
Corps, and reserve components, as well as the Defense Communications
Agency. Each of the team members was tasked by his or her parent
organization to ensure that its own interests were protected and that its

role in the war was properly showcased. Since the report could have a bearing on future allocation of defense resources, each organization wanted to make sure that its own programs received support.

The next nine months were to feel like the longest ones of my life. We spent more time writing about the war than we did fighting it. Although the war had been fought in the Middle East, the real battles—future budgets and missions—were to be waged in the halls of the Pentagon. The Defense Department's report to Congress would have a real impact on how the U.S. armed forces would be structured and funded in a changing world. With the end of the Cold War and the departure of the Soviet Union from the global scene, radical changes were inevitable in the U.S. defense establishment. That meant money and force-structure reductions, although the effective performance of a particular branch of the armed forces or its weapon systems in the Gulf War might translate into fewer such cutbacks for that branch and its weapons research and development programs.

The most contentious issues the team had to deal with were the effect and role of air power (air force and navy versus army and marine corps), the question of whether or not a true maritime campaign had been conducted (navy and marine corps versus air force and army), and the use of the phrase "hundred-hour war" (army versus everyone else). Each compromise made by the team had to be approved at senior levels, sometimes by the service secretary and the chief of staff. The value of air power generated the most heated debate, and the issue was not resolved for the report—to this day it remains a source of argument among the services.[1]

On the intelligence side, the contentious issues were between the CENTCOM directorate of intelligence and the DIA and between the CIA and the intelligence organizations of the Department of Defense. CENTCOM insisted that its version of the intelligence chapters and annexes be used, while the team believed that the Washington perspective was more appropriate for a report to the Congress. It was, after all, the secretary of defense's report to Congress, not CENTCOM's report. In the end, CENTCOM and the DIA were able to decide on language that both could accept. While civilian and military leaders in Washington and General Schwarzkopf, speaking for the theater commanders, agreed that intelligence support had been good overall, lower-level commanders (corps, divisions, carrier battle groups, and air wings) felt that intelligence support at tactical levels was lacking, sometimes severely.

Multiple versions of the report were produced. The first was an interim report sent to Congress, in both classified and unclassified forms, in July 1991. The final report was due by the end of the year, but the deadline was extended into 1992. The team produced a draft final report by November, which we all regarded as a quality product, a true account of the war written by officers who all had served in various services, units, locations, and command levels. The draft was coordinated with CENTCOM, who wanted its perspective to be the default position anytime there was a conflict. Differences in preferred wording were worked out, usually amicably, among professional military officers.

Then came the hard part. The report had to be coordinated through the Joint Chiefs of Staff (JCS) and the Office of the Secretary of Defense. Coordination through the JCS was fairly easy, since the service staffs had been intimately involved in the preparation of the draft and had provided the personnel to the report team. However, the OSD was another matter entirely. Whereas the JCS is composed almost totally of field-grade (major, lieutenant colonel, and colonel) or general officers, most hand-picked for their positions, the OSD is primarily made up of civilians. A large percentage of these officials are political appointees either who have no military experience or who owe their positions to the administration in office at the time. While most of the staff members in the OSD are conscientiously trying to do a good job, there is always the political agenda to be considered. And the coordination of the report to Congress on the war was no exception.

Every sentence, observation, conclusion, and recommendation of the report had to be looked at through a political optic. For example, one of the conclusions cited the poor capabilities of the Saudi military and civilian intelligence services. Such issues were included in the classified version but had been removed from the unclassified version. The OSD was concerned that if there were ever a leak of any of the judgments expressed in the classified version, we in the Defense Department might appear to be critical of a coalition ally. Of course we were being critical. This was a report from the Department of Defense to the Congress, not a political speech seeking Saudi approval of a foreign-policy issue. And indeed, if we wrote all classified documents taking into consideration a potential leak, we would never write anything worth reading.

After the final, fully coordinated report was completed in early 1992, I received a call from the CENTCOM director of intelligence, Gen. Jack Leide. As he had promised to do when the war was over, he asked what I wanted for my next assignment. I told him I had heard that he had been nominated for his second star and named as the new chief of the Defense Attaché System, managed by the DIA. He said that was true. I asked if he could arrange for me to be the first-ever air attaché to the U.S. embassy in Damascus. He said he would try to make that happen. I got orders the next month and went to Syria later that year.

I left the United States for the Middle East again on a happy note, for I had received word that Gen. Nabil Sa'id—the former Iraqi military attaché to the United States and my colleague in 1987 and 1988—might still be alive. Despite the reports of his execution in 1990, perhaps through some intrigue—it is Baghdad, after all—he had managed to escape the hangman's noose. I like to think so.

Epilogue

Is this the man that made the earth tremble, who shook kingdoms, who made the world like a desert and overthrew its cities, who did not let his prisoners go home?
Isaiah 14:16–17 (taunt against the king of Babylon)

All totaled, three hundred ninety Americans died in the Gulf War. Estimates of Iraqi dead range from one hundred twenty thousand to one hundred eighty thousand. Iraqi forces had been expelled from Kuwait, and the sheikhdom was restored—though still not a democracy, at least Kuwait was no longer under the thumb of Saddam Husayn. Iraq's programs for weapons of mass destruction had been dealt a severe setback, and the United Nations would attempt to complete the task of their destruction, with Iraq's agreement. Most of Iraqi airspace remained under coalition control.

Although Iraq's forces had been ejected from Kuwait and soundly defeated on the battlefield, Saddam Husayn remained (and, as of this writing, remains) in power in Baghdad. Almost immediately after the cessation of fighting between the coalition and Iraqi forces, there were two uprisings in Iraq—one from the Shi'a Muslims in the south and the other from the Kurds in the north. Both were put down brutally by the remnants of the Iraqi army. In fact, in the years since the end of the Gulf War, despite sanctions and shortages, the Iraqi armed forces are still a major military power in the region. The ability of these forces to reconstitute themselves is impressive.

The abuses and excesses of Saddam's internal security and intelligence services continue. American efforts to oust him appear to be disjointed, to lack resolve, and to have no clearly defined goals—and all of them have failed.

Since my return from Syria in early 1995, I have participated in some of these efforts. Most of the operations remain classified, although details of some have appeared in the press. Eventually, an Iraqi individual or a group of Iraqis will decide that they have had enough and will overthrow the dictator. Maybe then I will return to Baghdad and look up an old friend.

Notes

PROLOGUE

1. The nature of U.S. involvement with Iraq during the Iran-Iraq War became public knowledge and attracted media attention after Operation Desert Storm had ended. Official documents reveal the relationship: see U.S. Congress, Senate, Select Committee on Intelligence, *Report on the Nomination of Robert M. Gates,* 179–82; House, Congressman Gonzalez of Texas describing U.S. intelligence sharing with Iraq from 1984 to 1990, *Congressional Record,* 1109–11; Brent Scowcroft, "NSC/Deputies Committee Review," and tab A to that document; "Iraq: Options Paper," by Edward Gnehm and John Kelly, U.S. Department of State Memorandum for Brent Scowcroft, 16 May 1990, originally classified Secret.

2. The 1987 defense of Al-Basrah was reminiscent of the Iranian failed attempt to take the city in July 1982. After a series of Iranian victories in which Iraqi forces were ejected from Iranian territory, the Iraqis stopped the Iranians once the Iraqis were in the position of defending Iraqi territory, specifically Al-Basrah.

3. This relationship is described in Brian Shellum's *A Chronology of Defense Intelligence in the Gulf War: A Research Aid for Analysts,* prepared by the History Office of Defense Intelligence Agency in Washington, D.C., in 1997.

4. Designating the Directorate of Military Intelligence to conduct this relationship with the United States made sense. Military attachés are members of their nations' military intelligence service and are assigned to embassies to handle military-to-military contacts with host governments. An attaché is accredited to the host country's military intelligence service.

5. Throughout this book, the spelling of certain Arabic names differs from that commonly used by American journalists and scholars. With few exceptions, however, the author has followed the standard Arabic transliteration system used by the U.S. government's Board on Geographic Names. The reader will note that the surname of Saddam Husayn is rendered according to the BGN system, while the surname of King Hussein is spelled in the more popular form. Although in Arabic, the king's and Saddam's surnames are one and the same, for the purposes of this work they are spelled differently to avoid any confusion between the two leaders.

CHAPTER 1. IRAQ 1988

1. Wehr, *A Dictionary of Modern Written Arabic*, 67.

2. The goal of the Iraqi incursion was limited. Saddam wanted the Khomeini regime to stop its covert actions and renegotiate the Algiers Agreement.

3. The first and second "War of the Cities"—which took place in February 1984 and March–April 1985—involved air attacks on Baghdad and Tehran. In 1987 and 1988, the weapons were ballistic missiles.

4. Iraqi officers claimed that the German autobahn was the model for the Iraqi road system and that German consultants were involved in the design of the roads.

5. United Nations Document S/1995/864, Report of the Executive Chairman of the Special Commission, 11 October 1995, par. 41. Project 144 was the overall Iraqi program for the modification and production of missile systems. Subprojects included 144/2, the development of special (chemical and biological) warheads for the missiles, and 144/5, the testing of a three-stage missile system.

6. The description of "relatively minimal damage" here is meant in contrast to the effect of the normal thousand-kilogram (twenty-two hundred pounds) warhead carried on the standard Soviet-produced Scud missile used by the Iranians. These warheads were capable of leveling buildings.

7. The venue of the summit was later shifted from Baghdad to India because of the war.

8. In the U.S. intelligence community, the CIA is responsible for intelligence collection to support foreign policy and economic issues in response to the president and the National Security Council, while the DIA is charged with collection of information in response to the requirements of the secretary of defense, the Joint Chiefs of Staff, and military commanders. Each branch also has a small intelligence staff for service-specific needs and resource management.

9. See U.S. Congress, Senate, Select Committee on Intelligence, *Report on the Nomination of Robert M. Gates*, 179–82.

10. "U.S. Said to Have Threatened Use of Laser against French Satellite before 1991 Gulf War," *Inside Missile Defense*, 24 October 1997, 1.

11. In a story written by the Associated Press, the then-director of Central Intelligence, John Deutch, is reported to have acknowledged this intelligence community rule that forbids the use of the journalist role as a cover ("News Media Protest CIA Spy Policy," *Dubuque* (Iowa) *Telegraph Herald*, 22 February 1996).

12. Marshall Wiley, "Sanctions against Iraq: Let's Not Be Stupid," *Washington Post*, 20 August 1988.

13. Kuwait asked both the Soviet Union and the United States to protect its shipping. The U.S. decision to register the Kuwaiti ships under the American flag may have been largely an attempt to prevent expanded Soviet influence in the region.

14. While no empirical data exist to corroborate the theory, it appeared to us in the embassy that death banners existed in far greater numbers in the poorer sections of town, particularly the Shi'a sections, than in other, more affluent (and Sunni or Christian) areas of the city.

CHAPTER 2. INTERREGNUM

1. Iraq, unlike such Islamic states as Saudi Arabia and Iran, is a secular country and does not restrict women from working, driving, or serving in the armed forces. In fact, women have served as cabinet ministers and ambassadors.
2. U.S. Department of State, Office of the Historian, *American Foreign Policy: Current Documents*, 260.
3. Kimura Mitsuhiro, "Exclusive Interview with Udai Hussein," *Tokyo Kaleido-Scoop*, 10 June 1996.
4. See U.S. Department of State, "Iraqi Weapons of Mass Destruction Programs," 1–17.
5. See the DIA's memorandum "Iraq: Potential for Chemical Weapon Use" (February 1991), now declassified and placed on the Internet at the Defense Department's GulfLINK site (http://www.gulflink.osd.mil/declassdocs/dia/19970613/970613_dim37_91d_txt_0001.html).
6. Schwarzkopf, *It Doesn't Take a Hero*, 283.
7. See "Iraqi Weapons of Mass Destruction Programs," 1–17.
8. "Iraq Admits to U.N. It Built 'Supergun' with Nuclear Capability," *Washington Post*, 20 July 1991, A14.

CHAPTER 3. PRELUDE TO CONFLICT

1. Karabell, *Prelude to War*, 10.
2. Following the defeat of the Ottoman Empire in World War I, Iraq came under a British mandate. The British later established a kingdom in Iraq but maintained Kuwait as a separate British territory, mainly because of its excellent harbor. Kuwaiti-British relations dated back to a treaty signed in 1899, giving Britain responsibility for defense and foreign affairs. That status was reaffirmed in a 1913 British-Ottoman agreement; however, the agreement was never ratified.
3. The Shatt Al-'Arab, the waterway forming Iraq's border with Iran, had been blocked by sunken ships and unexploded ordnance since the beginning of the Iran-Iraq War in 1980. By way of comparison, Iran has 1,240 miles of shoreline on the Persian Gulf, while Iraq has only fifteen.
4. The geographic separation from the command headquarters and its area of responsibility has always been a problem for the CENTCOM intelligence directorate. Middle East specialists (officers with advanced degrees in

regional affairs and Arabic language ability) are reluctant to take an assignment to Tampa because they prefer to work directly in the region where their specialty itself is centered. Conversely, rather than specifically desiring to work on Middle East issues, many people seek to be assigned to CENTCOM because it provides a headquarters tour in a pleasant location in the United States.

5. The DIA study differed from the CENTCOM study in that it addressed the takeover of Kuwait, which the DIA judged could be done with five divisions. The CENTCOM analysis included moving a credible force to the Saudi border in preparation for a possible assault into the kingdom, which CENTCOM analysts thought would require eleven divisions. Both were correct.

6. Two other events colored our analysis. On 8 August, Iraq annexed Kuwait as its nineteenth province. On 14 August, in a surprise move Saddam Husayn ended Iraq's ongoing dispute with Iran by reinstating Iraq's adherence to the 1975 Algiers Agreement on the Shatt Al-'Arab.

CHAPTER 4. RIYADH

1. Saudi officials at the kingdom's embassy in Washington had for years sponsored radio programs targeted at converting Americans to Islam. Cash payments of as much as thirty-five thousand dollars were sometimes made to new converts, as well as all-expenses-paid trips to the holy sites in Saudi Arabia.

2. Al-Farsy, *Modernity and Tradition*, 59–61. The Saudi Arabian National Guard grew out of the Office of Jihad and Mujahidin (Holy War and Holy War Fighters), formed by King 'Abd Al-'Aziz in 1928. This organization was chartered by the king to provide a decent standard of living for the fighters who assisted him in his quest to unite the various tribal groupings in the Arabian Peninsula—by force, more often than not. Today's members are likely direct descendants of this original group and are considered extremely loyal to the monarchy.

3. King Fahd and Prince Sultan are two of seven brothers with the same mother, referred to as the "Sudayri Seven," a powerful grouping of potential future rulers of Saudi Arabia. The group is often at odds with the other sons of King 'Abd Al-'Aziz Al-Sa'ud, founder of the kingdom that bears his name.

4. When asked about the unequal distribution of wealth in the Arab world—for example, between Egypt with its large population, limited oil reserves, and staggering unemployment on one hand, and Saudi Arabia and the other Gulf states with their small populations, huge oil reserves, and thousands of expatriate workers and servants on the other—a Saudi major simply (and arrogantly) stated, "God meant for us to be rich."

CHAPTER 6. AMMAN

1. The League of Nations authorized the British mandate for Palestine and Iraq in 1922, to take effect in 1923. Syria and Lebanon were placed under French mandate. An earlier commission established by American president Woodrow Wilson had originally recommended that Syria be an American mandate. Although Faysal was first installed as king of Syria, he was ousted and placed in Iraq.

2. See Library of Congress, "U.S. Policy toward Iraq: 1980–1990," 26–27.

3. Prince Sultan, *Desert Warrior,* 399–400.

4. The Jordanian military attaché's work on behalf of Iraq was confirmed later by Saddam's chief of military intelligence, Brig. Gen. Wafiq Al-Samarra'i, after his defection to the West in 1994 ("Interview with Wafic Samarrai, Head of Iraqi Military Intelligence," *Frontline: The Gulf War,* Public Broadcasting System).

CHAPTER 7. THE SHEIKH AND THE COURIER

1. After the launch of the ground offensive in February 1991, the coalition had to move one and a half million gallons of water every day for the Iraqi prisoners of war, who numbered over eighty thousand.

CHAPTER 8. HAIL MARY AND THE POLITICS OF PLANNING

1. "Interview with Wafic Samarrai," *Frontline: The Gulf War.*

2. "Interview with Wafic Samarrai," *Frontline: The Gulf War.* General Al-Samarra'i also cites cooperation from the Pakistani intelligence service; however, this report is questionable, since Pakistan provided forces to the coalition. Those forces saw action on the northern Saudi border.

CHAPTER 9. LESSONS IN AIR POWER

1. Secretary Baker recounts his meeting with Tariq 'Aziz in great detail in *The Politics of Diplomacy,* 355–63.

2. The relationship between a Joint Force Air Component and U.S. Marine Corps aircraft is spelled out in a 1978 agreement between the air force and the marines. Marine commanders retain control of only the number of aircraft sorties required to directly support marine ground or amphibious operations. Sorties available above that amount are controlled by the JFACC.

3. Prince Sultan, *Desert Warrior,* 350.

CHAPTER 10. OF SCUDS AND PATRIOTS

1. Two Joint Chiefs of Staff documents declassified in late 1995 describe the inoculation program: JCS/J-4 information paper, "Anthrax and Botulinum Toxin Vaccination Plan for Operation Desert Shield," 5 October 1990; and JCS/J-3, "Warning Order for Biological Defense Program," 19 December 1990. Both are available on the Defense Department's GulfLINK Internet site at http://www.gulflink.osd.mil/declassdocs/jcs/19960117 (files e_0001.html and i_0001.html respectively).

2. See Friedman, *Desert Victory*. The Al-Husayn warhead was reduced from one thousand to two hundred fifty kilograms with a 15 percent increase in fuel load, for a range of six hundred fifty kilometers. The Al-'Abbas warhead was reduced to one hundred twenty-five kilograms and the fuel load increased by 30 percent for a range of eight hundred kilometers.

CHAPTER 11. BOB SIMON FINDS THE WAR

1. Kari is the French-designed computer system that linked and integrated Iraq's dissimilar air defense radars and command and control systems into one system. The name Kari is merely the French spelling of *Iraq* (*Irak*) in reverse.

CHAPTER 12. THE GROUND ASSAULT

1. In one instance, photography was in fact an accurate source of unit identification. The Iraqi 5th Mechanized Infantry Division was equipped with Chinese-made armored personnel carriers. Since it was the only unit in the Iraqi army with this particular vehicle, identification of the 5th Division from photography was possible.

2. Intelligence reports on the chemical weapons storage depot at Al-Khamisiyah were available as early as the Iran-Iraq War. The problem was retrieval and dissemination of the information because of the need to transliterate the Arabic script into the Roman alphabet, the standard script of the English language. Depending on the particular organizations and their own transliteration protocols, the name Al-Khamisiyah was spelled a number of different ways (or alternate names were used) among the various automated data bases. Although the U.S. government has a standard transliteration system (the U.S. Board on Geographic Names system), its use is not strictly enforced. A notable exception is the CIA, who uses the system reasonably consistently in its reporting. Although Congress mandated compliance with the standard in 1997, little progress has been evident.

3. See the item "Second Decontamination Site Identified" in the Defense Intelligence Agency's "Persian Gulf Situation Report" (16 September 1990), available on the Internet at http://www.artbell.com/mirror/gulflink/950719ep.txt).

4. Avigdor Haselkorn, "Saddam's Secret Weapon Is Worse Than Imagined," *Los Angeles Times,* 10 October 1997.

5. "Interview with Wafic Samarrai," *Frontline: The Gulf War.*

CHAPTER 16. TITLE V

1. During the writing of this book, I submitted drafts to several general officers who had played central roles in the war. Advocates of air power say I have been too "pro-ground," while generals from the army and the marines say I have been too parochial to the air force since I was an air force officer.

Bibliography

Al-Farsy, Fouad. *Modernity and Tradition: The Saudi Equation*. London: Keegan Paul, 1990.

Baker, James Addison. *The Politics of Diplomacy: Revolution, War, and Peace, 1989–1992*. New York: Putnam, 1995.

Friedman, Norman. *Desert Victory: The War for Kuwait*. Annapolis, Md.: Naval Institute Press, 1991.

Gordon, Michael R., and Bernard E. Trainor. *The Generals' War: The Inside Story of the Conflict in the Gulf*. Boston: Little, Brown, 1995.

Hosenball, Mark. "The Odd Couple: How George Bush Helped Create Saddam Hussein." *New Republic* 206.22 (1 June 1992): 27.

Kaplan, Robert D. *The Arabists: The Romance of an American Elite*. New York: Free Press, 1993.

Karabell, Zachary. *Prelude to War: U.S. Policy toward Iraq 1988–1990*. Cambridge: Harvard University, Kennedy School of Government, 1994.

Karsh, Efraim, and Inari Rautsi. *Saddam Hussein: A Political Biography*. New York: Free Press, 1991.

Khaled [Khalid] Bin Sultan, Prince. *Desert Warrior: A Personal View of the Gulf War by the Joint Forces Commander*. New York: HarperCollins, 1995.

Library of Congress. "U.S. Policy toward Iraq: 1980–1990." *Congressional Research Service Report for Congress*, 26 June 1992.

Miller, Judith, and Laurie Mylroie. *Saddam Hussein and the Crisis in the Gulf*. New York: Times Books, 1990.

Oberdorfer, Don. "Mixed Signals in the Middle East." *Washington Post Magazine*, 17 March 1991.

Powell, Colin L., with Joseph E. Persico. *My American Journey*. New York: Random House, 1995.

Schwarzkopf, H. Norman, with Peter Petre. *It Doesn't Take a Hero: General H. Norman Schwarzkopf: The Autobiography*. New York: Bantam, 1992.

Sciolino, Elaine. *The Outlaw State: Saddam Hussein's Quest for Power and the Gulf Crisis*. New York: Wiley and Sons, 1991.

Scowcroft, Brent. "NSC/Deputies Committee Review of PCC Paper on Iraq." National Security Council Memorandum, 18 May 1990, originally classified Secret.

U.S. Congress. House. *Congressman Gonzalez of Texas describing U.S. intelligence sharing with Iraq from 1984 to 1990*. 102d Cong., 2d sess., *Congressional Record* (9 March 1992), vol. 138, pt. 32.

————. Senate. Select Committee on Intelligence. *Report on the Nomination of Robert M. Gates to be Director of Central Intelligence*. Executive Report 102-19, 24 October 1991.

U.S. Department of Defense. *Conduct of the Persian Gulf War: A Final Report to Congress*. Washington, D.C.: Department of Defense, 1992.

U.S. Department of State. "Iraqi Weapons of Mass Destruction Programs." U.S. Government White Paper, 13 February 1998.

————. Office of the Historian. *American Foreign Policy: Current Documents*. Washington, D.C.: Department of State, 1991.

U.S. News and World Report. *Triumph without Victory: The Unreported History of the Persian Gulf War*. New York: Times Books, 1992.

Wehr, Hans. *A Dictionary of Modern Written Arabic*. Edited by J. Milton Cowan. Ithaca, N.Y.: Spoken Language Services, 1971.

Index

About the Author

Rick Francona is a retired Air Force intelligence officer and Middle East specialist. In addition to his role as the lead U.S. military interpreter during the Gulf War and a principal author of the report to Congress on the conflict, he served throughout the Middle East with the defense department and national intelligence agencies. The author lives in Oregon.